Memories

Looking back with the Rainy Day Writers

Want more Rainy Day Writers?
Visit the Rainy Day Writers' website at
https://sites.google.com/site/rainydaywriters2
or use the QR code below.

Memories

Looking back with the Rainy Day Writers

Rainy Day Writers
Cambridge, Ohio

Memories
ISBN-13: 978-1727186703
ISBN-10: 1727186702

Memories. Copyright 2018, CreateSpace. Printed and bound in the United States of America. All rights reserved. No part of this book may be used or reproduced in any manner whatsoever — except by a reviewer who may quote brief passages in a review — without written permission from the publisher.

RAINY DAY WRITERS
CAMBRIDGE, OHIO

Contents

8   *ACKNOWLEDGMENTS*
9   *EDITOR'S NOTE*

CHRISTMAS PAST

10   The Perfect Gift
     BETSY TAYLOR
13   Coal for Christmas
     SAMUEL D. BESKET
16   The First Dickens Christmas
     BOB LEY
19   No Cussing on Christmas
     JUDY SIMCOX
22   "Merry Christmas, Rosie"
     HARRIETTE MCBRIDE ORR
25   Learning My ABCs
     BEVERLY WENCEK KERR
27   The Christmas Train
     RICK BOOTH
30   The Box in Brown Paper
     MARK COOPER

STORES AND BUSINESSES

32   My First Job
     BETSY TAYLOR
35   The Berwick
     BOB LEY
37   Look at Your Door
     SAMUEL D. BESKET

40   Remembering Midtown News
     RICK BOOTH
43   Gray's General Store
     MARK COOPER
46   Sidewalk Sales in Cambridge
     MARK COOPER
48   Chicken Feed
     BEVERLY WENCEK KERR
50   Fired from My First Job
     MARTHA F. JAMAIL
53   A Fun Place
     BOB LEY
55   Full Circle
     SAMUEL D. BESKET
57   Aunt Ruth's Store
     BETSY TAYLOR
60   Don't Lose Your Marbles
     BETSY TAYLOR
63   Sandman
     BEVERLY WENCEK KERR
66   A Guys' World
     JOY L. WILBERT ERSKINE

RAILROADS AND COAL

68   Memories of 7819 Railroad Avenue
     JOY L. WILBERT ERSKINE

71 The Telegrapher and the Comet
RICK BOOTH

74 The Land of Hope
BEVERLY WENCEK KERR

76 Here It Comes
SAMUEL D. BESKET

78 Name Badges
BOB LEY

SNOWS TO REMEMBER

80 The Blizzard of '78
BETSY TAYLOR

84 White Stuff
BOB LEY

86 In the Snowbanks
JOY L. WILBERT ERSKINE

88 Big Snows I Have Known
JUDY SIMCOX

91 Melting Snow
BEVERLY WENCEK KERR

93 My First Blizzard
MARTHA F. JAMAIL

95 Mom, I Tore My Pants Again
SAMUEL D. BESKET

97 Stranded
HARRIETTE MCBRIDE ORR

THE "OLD COUNTRY"

101 The "Boys"
BOB LEY

103 An Immigrant's Story
MARTHA F. JAMAIL

107 Chan Gee, Laundryman or Tea Merchant?
RICK BOOTH

111 Babushka Power
BEVERLY WENCEK KERR

113 The Fourth of July in Kipling, Ohio
HARRIETTE MCBRIDE ORR

ON THE FARM

116 Harvest in 1955
BETSY TAYLOR

119 I Never Lived on a Farm
JUDY SIMCOX

122 A Menace of a Rooster
HARRIETTE MCBRIDE ORR

125 Summer Visits
JOY L. WILBERT ERSKINE

128 Strawberry Time
BEVERLY WENCEK KERR

130 Grace Had a Little Lamb
MARK COOPER

132 Hayin' by "City Boys"
BOB LEY

WHERE WE DINED

134 Mom's Kitchen
JOY L. WILBERT ERSKINE

136 My First Time Eating Out
MARK COOPER

138 Eateries
BOB LEY

141 Bennett's Drive-In
BEVERLY WENCEK KERR

Teacher Tales

144 My Aunt Margaret McBride
HARRIETTE MCBRIDE ORR

147 Brain vs. Calculator
MARTHA F. JAMAIL

149 What I Learned
BOB LEY

151 My Kindergarten Report Card
MARK COOPER

153 Remembering Andre Odebrecht
RICK BOOTH

156 Sprechen Sie Deutsch?
JOY L. WILBERT ERSKINE

159 High School Journalism
BEVERLY WENCEK KERR

161 My Favorite Teachers
MARTHA F. JAMAIL

168 A Writer's Inspiration
BETSY TAYLOR

Odds and Ends

172 Similarities of the Past
SAMUEL D. BESKET

175 The Place to Be
BETSY TAYLOR

178 What Happened to "Bill"?
BOB LEY

180 My Own Little Miracle
JUDY SIMCOX

183 Church at Seneca Lake
BOB LEY

185 I'm from Buffalo
SAMUEL D. BESKET

188 *Photo Credits*

Acknowledgments

Thank you, Friends! It's the feedback and acknowledgment we've received from each of our past publications that has kept us, the Rainy Day Writers, on track to produce yet another book. In response to positive feedback from previous stories of local reminiscence, we decided to create and publish a collection of tales specifically of that nature, found herein.

Besides our responsive readers, the special local businesses listed below have been particularly helpful to us, and we recognize them gratefully here. Please patronize these generous friends and neighbors who support the Rainy Day Writers in so many ways:

Crossroads Library
Cambridge Copy Shop
Cambridge Heights Apartments
Cambridge News[*]
Cambridge Packaging[*]
Dickens Welcome Center[*]
Guernsey County History Museum
Lady Jane's Mercantile[*]
Modern Movements[*]
Mr. Lee's Restaurant[*]
Penny Court[*]
Riesbeck's[*]
Shafer Insurance Agency Inc.
The Daily Jeffersonian[*]
The Towne House Gifts and Interiors[*]

* Book sales location.

Editor's Note

Over the years, we Rainy Day Writers have seen that stories about shared memories of our local past strike a chord with the reading public. As much as we enjoy writing about the way things used to be, readers seem to enjoy taking in those same shared recollections. We therefore decided this year to target memory's sweet spot with this, our latest book.

Most of the stories told herein come from our memories of local happenings, though not all do. Several of our members spent their formative years elsewhere, so a bit of life in the East, the West, and even the Deep South is present here as well. The common thread of life in the middle of the twentieth century – and sometimes even earlier – runs through it all.

To organize our thoughts, we selected several themes that most people, in the course of life, remember distinctly and often fondly. Everyone has a favorite story of a snowfall or the way Christmas was celebrated. Then there are the stores and businesses from long ago, most of which are gone now. Whole industries like glassware, passenger rail, and coal came and went. Schools and teachers came to mind. The ethnic ties to lands across the sea were fresher back then, too. Further to that point, a closeness to the land itself – the experience of farm life – was once more common than it is today. They're good memories all.

Martha Jamail served as the main editing arbiter of article consistency and style. It has been my pleasure to compose this book for publication. The Guernsey County History Museum deserves much credit, too, for generously sharing many of the photos filling pages with historical tidbits between articles.

I and the other Rainy Day Writers hope you enjoy this book!

–Rick Booth, Composing Editor

The Perfect Gift

BY BETSY TAYLOR

No purchase required.

    "Christmas," grumbled Jenny. Another season of stewing over gift selection, of listening to her brother, Rand, call her "Grinch" and "Scrooge," and another season of present pressure.

    Jenny had saved her allowance and baby-sitting money to make purchases but the dilemma of what to give each person on her list drove her nuts.

    "Don't be such a whiny baby," mocked Rand. "It's not that hard to figure this out. Here's the Kohl's advertisement. Just scan through it and pick out a few things. Look, there's even a sale." Rand tossed the flyer on Jenny's desk. "Oh yeah, that's where I already bought my gifts, so some of those are taken," he called over his shoulder as he dashed off to his volunteer job.

    "Thanks a heap," Jenny growled. As she thumbed through the flyer's shiny pages, she became even more discouraged. Grandma Jane didn't need another set of gloves, scarf, and hat. Mom didn't want another kitchen gadget. Dad could use another sweater… maybe. Rand might like a set of hand weights. Oh, wait. He'd returned a set of those last Christmas.

    As a last resort, she could do what she had done last year – include a receipt with each gift so they could be returned or exchanged.

    Through the day, Jenny pondered her dilemma. Finally, she decided to go back to her default strategy – coupons. When she was much younger, Jenny had decorated index cards with promises. For Grandma Jane, she had drawn a stack of pancakes with the promise of three breakfasts for just the two of them. Mom's coupon promised Jenny as a walking partner on ten outings. Dad had been given the promise of three golf games caddied by Jenny, who even included her "expert" advice. A coupon gave Rand the guarantee of bathing Foxy, his beloved Jack Russell terrier, three times.

Those gifts seemed so juvenile, but, at least, they'd be useful and appreciated. Jenny assembled her stack of cards, markers, and glitter pens. Worn out, she decided to tackle the project first thing the next morning.

That night her dreams were unsettled. Disturbing images followed each other through her sleep. Jenny tossed and turned, finally getting up just before dawn. Despite her restlessness, she awoke alert. Enthusiastically, she went to her desk and dove into her project. She lavishly decorated each index card, then wrapped each packet with care.

On Christmas morning, Jenny's family exchanged gifts. Hers were opened last. As Jenny handed out each packet, she glowed with excitement.

Grandma Jane clapped her hands with delight when she saw that a donation in her name had been made to a clean water project in Appalachia. Mom was thrilled with her contribution to the Salvation Army's food program. Dad's eyes watered when he saw his gift to the local homeless shelter. At last, Rand pulled the ribbon on his gift.

"Jenny! This is super! In fact, it's perfect. The animal shelter will make the best use of this money. And your offer to volunteer… well, what can I say? Well, except, thank you."

Later that day, Rand asked, "I guess all your stewing around about presents worked out. What made you come up with such a great idea?"

"The truth is, it came to me in a nightmare."

Barely Changed...

With the exception of the door at center left, the Salvation Army building on Dewey Avenue in Cambridge looks nearly the same today as it did in this 1948 sesquicentennial celebration booklet photo.

Photo courtesy of the Guernsey County History Museum.

Coal for Christmas

BY SAMUEL D. BESKET

Coal – Don't start winter without it.

A cold wind blew snow against the window as Mary stared at the drifts building outside her home. The fluffy white powder swirled as it covered the tracks left by the mailman minutes earlier. There was a time when she hated the winter, but now, in her old age, she had a warm house and a family to keep her comfortable. Her daydreaming was interrupted by her five-year-old granddaughter running into the room crying.

"Margot, Margot, why are you crying?"

Margot ran to her and collapsed into Mary's lap, her fiery red hair all a frizzle.

"Come on Margot, it can't be that bad."

"Sammy said I was getting a lump of coal for Christmas, not a doll house," she shouted. "He said I was a bad girl."

"Now, now, stop your crying, Sweetie, you know Sammy likes to tease little girls. You know, when I was a little girl, we got coal for Christmas one year and were glad we did."

A teary-eyed Margot looked up, "Really, Grandma? You were glad you got coal?"

"Yes, we did, and it's time you and your cousins heard the story. After all, Grandma is not getting any younger." She could see Sammy and his brothers peeking through the crack in the door, wondering what Margot was telling her.

"Danny, Sammy, Tommy, come in here boys. I know you're hiding outside the door." Slowly, the door opened and the boys sheepishly walked in.

"Sit," Mary said as she pointed to a place in front of the fireplace. The look on her face told the boys they better do as she asked. "I have a story to tell you kids about the time we got coal for Christmas."

"You got coal for Christmas, Grandma?" little Tommy asked.

"It was a long, long time ago, Tommy, long before you boys or your mother was born. Your great-grandpa George was a coal miner. He and my mother lived in a company house on a hill overlooking Leatherwood Creek. In January of 1937, there was a great flood in the Leatherwood Valley. I remember how it flooded all the mines, and washed away many of the miner's homes. Since we lived on a hill, our home was spared."

"Times were hard, and most of the miners moved away, but my parents stayed. That winter was hard and cold, then my father contracted the flu. By Christmas, they had used up all their savings. Remember, there wasn't any help for poor families like there is today. I was just five years old, and I remember Mom moved all of us into one room to keep warm – this room we are in now. We had just enough coal to last until Christmas."

"On Christmas Eve, Mom bundled me up and we walked to candlelight services at the Methodist Church in Lore City. After the service, as we were walking home, we saw a huge black blob in our back yard. As we got closer, we could tell it was a pile of coal. How it got there we don't know, but it was enough to last until spring."

"Did Santa bring it?" Danny shouted.

"We don't know, Danny, we just called it a gift from Jesus. You see, children, coal isn't necessarily a bad thing like you hear on television. For us, it was a lifesaver, that cold winter years ago."

"Now boys… listen to me, and I mean listen. If you continue to tease Margot, you won't get a lump of coal for Christmas, you'll get that paddle hanging on the wall. Just ask your mom, she is well acquainted with it."

ℜDѠℙ

History Preserved at HO Scale...

Black Top Mine, shown accurately modeled here on the Guernsey Valley Model Railroad Club's enormous track layout, was one of the many coal mines operating locally in the early twentieth century.

Photo courtesy of the Guernsey County History Museum, Adair Collection.

The First Dickens Christmas

BY BOB LEY

We call it a Dickens of a Christmas!

Like so many small towns, downtown Cambridge had started to decline. My wife, Sue, and I were talking about solutions to the problem. We narrowed down our plans for attracting visitors downtown to doing something with a Dickens theme.

Our original thoughts for Dickens Victorian Village were a series of life-size paintings of Dickens scenes to be attached to the street lampposts downtown. We had an art guild in Cambridge. The members could be asked to help paint the scenes.

Sue walked into my menswear store one day as I was dressing a mannequin for display. The thought hit her, "Why not use real scenes?" she asked. "We could make the scenes three dimensional. How much would mannequins cost?"

"Way too much! Many thousands," I told her. But I was a little bit intrigued. "Let me see what I can design," I said.

A few weeks later I had designed and built a prototype mannequin that could be posed. The biggest problem was mannequins needed heads and faces! Martha Jamail happened into the store one day. She was head of the local art guild and is an accomplished artist. After explaining what I needed, Martha took the ball and ran. Gathering together a group of fellow artists, after a lot of trial and error, they came up with the first faces, which were incredible. Work began in earnest.

Bob Bruner, at the vocational school in Buffalo, volunteered his class to build the framework for a hundred mannequins! Jonett Haberfield signed on as the go-to girl, working many hours a week getting the word out, organizing, and being a one-woman dynamo. Cindy Arent gathered a team to dress and pose more than a hundred mannequins, doing an incredible job even to this day! Lindy Thaxton came up with a way to pose the hands, making the figures much more realistic. Carl Beynon built more than 30 stands to go around the light poles so the scenes could be seen from the street.

Then came the day of reckoning: Move Out Day! We estimated it would be an all-day job to get the scenes out and placed. The media let the public know we needed help and literally hundreds of people showed up. Trucks with trailers, more than we could ever use, arrived. In less than two hours we were done!

The excitement downtown during that first Christmas was palpable. Visitors came from miles away, all with nice things to say about the efforts of our volunteers. Most could not believe a town our size could do this without professional help. Our downtown had the busy look of years earlier!

The most rewarding part was the enthusiasm of the volunteers. Every year they suggest something new and exciting. One year we purchased two very nice horse-drawn carriages to add to the atmosphere. The city added well done, clean, public restrooms for our visitors' convenience.

Grant Hafley and Joel Losego presented a proposal for a unique lighting of the court house. It would involve timing the lighting, thousands of lights, to music. It has proven to be a huge crowd-pleaser. Many visitors are on the grounds every evening to see the display, regardless of the temperature!

The first Dickens Christmas was a bit primitive compared to later ones, but for many, it has become a part of the Christmas tradition. It has developed into something Sue and I could never have imagined! It's been an amazing journey!

Down by the Railroad Tracks...

In 1910, dozens of women sewed the "Guernsey Overall" in this Cambridge Roofing Company-owned factory. Note the railroad tracks visible through the windows. This factory was located at the south end of Second Street in Cambridge. It looked "Dickensian!"

Photo courtesy of the Guernsey County History Museum.

No Cussing on Christmas

BY JUDY SIMCOX

Santa was a family affair.

I sometimes feel like I grew up long ago, in a galaxy far, far away. It really was New Jersey, and I lived there from the time I was six until I was sixteen. My parents had eight children when all was said and done, six of them younger than me. In New Jersey, the oldest separated from the upper end of the line to join the navy, and the youngest didn't appear at the lower end until we moved to Ohio. My mother stayed at home during those years, and may indeed have gone off her rocker a time or two, although all was well when she was older (and all of us were gone. . . more or less). A particularly hectic time must have been Christmas.

My dad put strings of lights outside with a staple gun, the lights with the big bulbs that, if one went bad, the whole string went off. He actually had the struggles with tangles that were the source of so much merriment in the funny papers. He may have had some help from my brothers, but I didn't pay much attention. I tried to help my mother.

Of course, I only helped with things she assigned to me, like keeping the younger ones out from underfoot, or things I wanted to do, like frost sugar cookies and lick the utensils . . . just me if I could manage it, or mostly me if I had to share. My mother made a gingerbread house when I was about seven. I have photographic proof somewhere, but she only did it once that I recall. We tried a couple of times later, when I received some useful lessons in precision and patience.

I don't know who helped her wrap all the gifts she assembled for seven kids, plus stockings. We actually got oranges in the toes of our stockings, topped off mostly by socks. The stockings were more or less the size of real woolen socks, and actually may have been. I remember holding my finger on half tied bows, but not being privy to others' "surprises." My dad did a good deal of assembling, too, of bikes and trikes and dollhouses.

I remember trying to be staunchly loyal to my parents and bravely cheerful upon receiving "cowgirl" regalia when my brothers received "cowboy" outfits, with chaps and six-guns and hats that looked real, not like party hats. I don't think I knew any cuss words at that time, but I probably would have saved them for later if I had.

One Christmas I received twin baby dolls, and my older brother, two years older than I, pitched a fit sufficient to induce my parents to gently coax the boy doll away from me and give it to him. What did he want with a baby doll? Looking back, the Spanish Inquisition comes to mind. I don't recall ever seeing him play with it. Maybe he just wanted it because babies were coming into the family pretty regularly, and he wanted to get the feel of it. Or maybe he wanted to do to the doll what he couldn't do to the baby, like sit on it or swirl it in the toilet. My brother wasn't evil, he was just the firstborn, and after my next brother and I came along, he may have felt like he was being chased by a pack of hounds. In fact, he told me once about a recurring dream where furry creatures were chasing him chanting, "I'm gonna maus it," only they were flying monkeys, not hounds.

I remember the time we had to hurriedly "undecorate" the tree, a blue spruce, and hustle it out, to be replaced by a scotch pine, because my youngest brother (in New Jersey) was wildly allergic. I also remember when my mom made a plum pudding that went over like a – plum pudding.

The days when all those kids were out of school and totally Christmas crazy must have been – what's the word? Awful? Good times!

On the Silver Screen...

William Boyd (1895 - 1972) was born in Hendrysburg, Belmont County, but he grew up in Cambridge before moving to Oklahoma as a teen. He considered Cambridge his home town. His Hollywood silent film career began in 1920. He first played the role of Hopalong Cassidy in the 1935 film *Hop-a-Long Cassidy*. Audiences loved his good-guy cowboy character. In the next 20 years, he made about 70 more movies playing America's favorite movie Western hero, though he always wore a black hat.

Poster by Paramount via Wikimedia Commons.

"Merry Christmas, Rosie"

BY HARRIETTE MCBRIDE ORR

A surprise on freedom's trail.

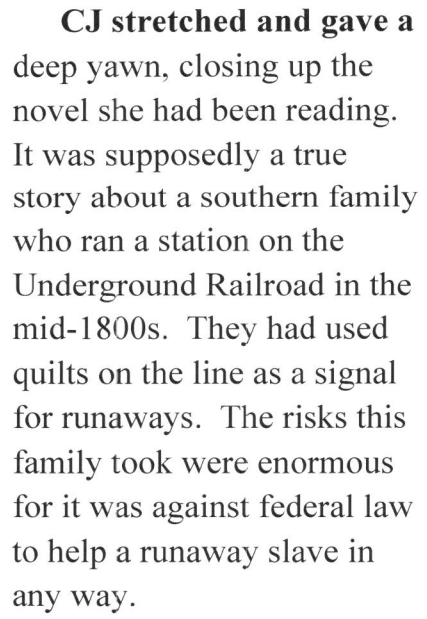

CJ stretched and gave a deep yawn, closing up the novel she had been reading. It was supposedly a true story about a southern family who ran a station on the Underground Railroad in the mid-1800s. They had used quilts on the line as a signal for runaways. The risks this family took were enormous for it was against federal law to help a runaway slave in any way.

CJ had been told stories of her great-grandmother Carnes' grandfather, Sam Craig, running an Underground Railroad station right here in Cambridge, on the southeast corner of the Public Square at 800 Wheeling Avenue. He was a wool dealer maintaining a mercantile store at this site, with his family home upstairs. Stories were that he hid runaways in the large feed bins in the stable at the rear of the store, with his wife Maggie feeding and tending to their needs. No one else, not even family, knew that this was taking place. The feed bins had doors in the back that opened up into the tack room where runaways could spend time when no one was around. Most often there was just one passenger, man or woman, but sometimes a whole family rested there.

CJ thought about the one

story she had heard many times, about a slave named Rosie. When Rosie was brought to this Cambridge safe house she was very much with child, and tired from running and hiding from the men and dogs sent after them. Her husband, Gustas, had boosted her up in a tall tree and then ran, leading the men away from her. The Craigs had decided to let Rosie stay until her husband hopefully caught up with her.

It was good that the weather was mild for December, for there was no heat source in the tack room.

Maggie made sure Rosie was warm enough by bringing her feather ticks and down comforters, as well as warming pans with hot coals and bricks from their fireplace. The tack room was lit by day with windows high up near the roof.

Rosie fretted about not having anything to do. "Miz Maggie, I'm good with a needle. Do you have any sewing I might do for you?"

"I certainly do, Rosie. I'll bring some down and make up a sewing basket."

As the days drew on, it became Christmas week. Rosie was finding it hard to get around. She had just finished mending a pair of pants when she felt a sharp pain and the warm rush of wetness running down her legs. "My lands," she said out loud. "I'm gonna have this baby. Oh, lordy." Just as another pain started, Maggie knocked on the door.

"Oh, Miz Maggie, my time has come."

"Don't you worry, Rosie. I've delivered lots of babies. Let's get you comfortable, then I'll run and get the things we need."

Maggie soon returned with night clothes, blankets, towels and a wash basin. Her husband built a fire outside telling the help that she was tending a sick horse.

It was Christmas Eve and Rosie labored into the night. Trying all the while to be quiet, Rosie was soon exhausted.

"Rosie, I can see the head now. Just one more push…PUSH! And here he is. Look, he's a beautiful baby boy!"

Maggie held the newborn up by his feet, and swatted his behind. A strong cry burst forth from his lungs. After cleaning and wrapping him in warm flannel, Maggie placed the sobbing child in his mother's arms. "Now, Rosie," she said, "I have a surprise for you."

Maggie opened the door and there, lo and behold, stood Rosie's husband, Gustas. Quickly he ran to Rosie, enfolding her and the baby in a loving hug. With tears running down his cheeks, he sobbed while rocking them back and forth.

"Thank you, Jesus, thank you. I'm here, darlin', I'm here."

"Merry Christmas," Maggie whispered, while quietly shutting the door.

This story always touched CJ's heart. She was so proud of her grandparents and was always left wondering just how many souls they had helped to freedom.

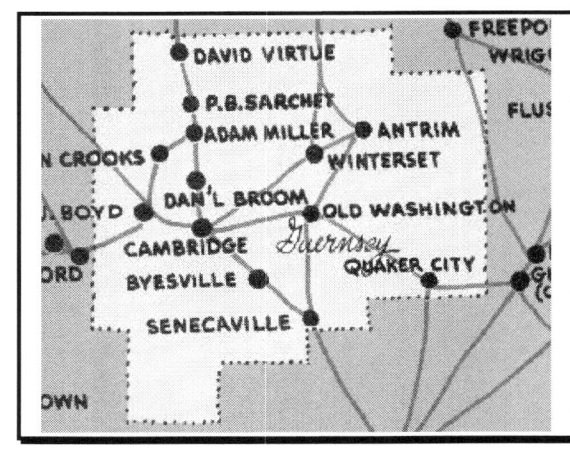

Guernsey County was once a key part of the Pre-Civil War escaped-slave-smuggling network known as the Underground Railroad. Located just 50 miles from slave state Virginia (now West Virginia), many a freedom-seeker made part of their way toward Canada here.

Learning My ABCs

BY BEVERLY WENCEK KERR

Chalk it up.

Mom always wanted to be a teacher, so early in my life she tried to provide ways of learning, even though there wasn't much money available. We moved from place to place during my first six years, and for me there was always something to enjoy. Friends appeared no matter where we lived.

At the age of six, we moved to 321 North 4th Street in Cambridge. We rented half of a house. Perhaps the nearness of Lofland School, just one block away, gave Dad and Mom a good reason to move there. Mom walked me to school for a few days, but shortly afterwards allowed me to walk home with friends.

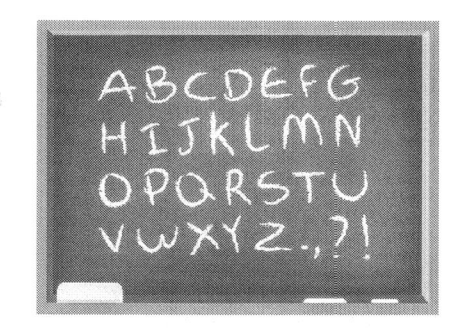

Many evenings Dad would give me a dime to go down to Galliher's Ice Cream after school. For that dime, a friend and I could both get an ice cream cone and sit on the stools by the counter. Sometimes we whirled the stools around as we licked our ice cream. Those were happy and tasty days.

On the weekends, Mom would walk with me to the Guernsey County Library. I didn't have any books of my own, but it certainly pleased me to take home two or three new-to-me books each week. Mom enjoyed reading to me and I began my love of books.

Christmas is always an exciting time for a child, and

mine was no exception. What would Santa leave? Would he find me since we moved? In a corner of the room, my mind still pictures our small Christmas tree with an angel on the top.

On Christmas morning, beside the tree sat a small desk with a chalkboard attached.

A teddy bear rested in the seat, just waiting for a hug. But the blackboard wasn't just an ordinary blackboard. It had the alphabet printed around the edge! This was an exciting moment for me because I enjoyed writing in the first grade and now had a place to practice at home.

No paper wasted now. An eraser made it possible to write and erase letters and words when desired.

Soon the alphabet could be recited not only forwards, but backwards as well. What fun to recite to my teachers, and my parents. Of course, the other students weren't very impressed, but that didn't bother me. All that mattered was my chalkboard gave me a place to write.

Who knows, perhaps that chalkboard planted the first seed to my becoming a writer today. Mom tried hard to make me the best I could be.

At the 19th Century's End...

The Lofland School, also known as the Fourth Street School, narrowly survived an 1899 fire on the coldest day ever recorded in Ohio. It was 32 degrees below zero in Cambridge. The record was set at 39 below in Perry County that day. That record still stands today.

The Christmas Train

BY RICK BOOTH

Was that Santa blowing the horn?

I was probably four years old when Santa first brought me a train – not a full-sized one, of course, but a good-sized electric set that ran around the living room floor. I don't recall having asked Santa for it, but I was delighted he'd left it. The set was rather large as model trains go. It was an "O-gauge" system, much larger than the smaller "HO" sets which were also popular at the time.

A black, cubic, metal transformer box controlled the train. Just turn its dial left to go forward, or right to back up. And then there were the switches. This train didn't just run in a circle. It could choose a left or a right path at a couple of switch points off the main loop. The switches were set by hand, of course, so the trick was to physically race the train to the switches between loops around the track to make it change course.

It didn't take me long to notice that my father was nearly as excited about the train set as I was. He taught me how to set the cars on the track and link them. I learned that too much speed on a curve caused derailments. Sometimes they were accidental, and sometimes I crashed things for fun. The train always survived. Tinsel, though, didn't. Dropping a strand from the Christmas tree onto the live track always brought an incendiary flash and crackle. That was fun, too.

The train set stayed up, congesting the living room floor, for nearly a month before going into temporary retirement. Dad assured me that someday we'd set it up again.

True to his word, my father helped construct the train set a few days before Christmas the next year. As I went to bed on Christmas Eve, I wondered what Santa might bring. Among other things, the next morning I discovered the kind old man had brought more track, switches, a trestle, some extra boxcars, and a special sort of fluid I could drop into the engine's smokestack to make it puff like a real locomotive. Dad seemed as delighted as I was with the railroad gift. I'm sure I logged more time playing with the set that year than Dad did, but he wasn't far behind.

For the next several years, each Christmas the set went up, and Santa made modifications and additions in the night. He was quite the engineer! It was so thoughtful of him to spend time redesigning the system while reindeer waited on our roof.

As I grew older and perhaps a bit wiser, I had my suspicions about the relationship between my father, Santa, and the train. I'll never forget the Christmas Eve I was tucked into bed, only to be awakened in the wee hours by the long blast of a horn sound I'd never heard before. It seemed to come from inside the house. As I went downstairs the next morning, there was my father, taking pictures and beaming next to the latest additions to the electric train set. There was now a second engine on the system. Suspiciously, he showed me that there was a way to make the new engine blow its horn. It wasn't particularly obvious that the engine could do that, but somehow Dad just knew.

In retrospect, I don't know whose eyes showed more delight on those Christmas mornings more than fifty years ago – my father's or mine. We shared the model railroad set and the joy of its runs and its wrecks together. Despite Santa's midnight slip of the horn, he was a wonderful engineer – of both trains and the bonds of fathers and sons.

Big Boys, Big Toys...

In the mid-1970s, a local group of model train enthusiasts set out to build a giant HO scale model railroad, dubbing it the Guernsey Valley Railroad. Over 40 years later, it is the largest such layout in the state, reproducing local historic railroad scenes in exquisite detail. The above photo of early construction was taken in 1975. Today, the layout spans most of the top floor of the Colley Block building at the corner of Wheeling Avenue and Seventh Street in Cambridge. Historic scenes along the tracks include area coal mines and villages.

Photo courtesy of the Guernsey County History Museum, Adair Collection

The Box in Brown Paper

BY MARK COOPER

Sometimes art is disposable.

Christmas Eve and an excited little boy – now that's a combination to induce panic in any mom. The year I was seven, I must have been particularly energetic on Christmas Eve. My big brother no doubt sensed Mom's need to have a few "boy-free" hours as she worked non-stop, cleaning and cooking for the family festivities planned for the next day.

My brother invited me upstairs to his room. There, on the floor, lay the most ginormous, gift-wrapped box I had ever seen. Instead of being wrapped in paper printed in a traditional holiday design, this mammoth box was covered in plain brown paper, held in place with duct tape and baling twine.

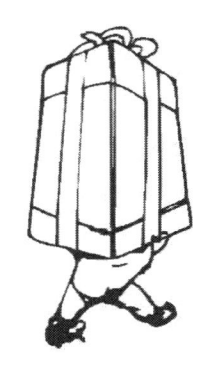

"Who is that for?" I asked excitedly.

"You'll have to wait until tomorrow to find out."

No amount of pleading on my part convinced my brother to disclose who would be the recipient of the gift, but he did explain why he had called me to his room. "This brown paper is too plain. Can you draw pictures on it so it looks nice under the tree?"

I agreed to undertake decorating the paper. I ran downstairs to grab a box of Crayolas. Soon, scenes of Christmas trees, snow men, and who knows what else, began transforming the gift wrap from brown and boring into a one-of-a-kind masterpiece.

The next morning, the box took up a large space on the floor, next to the tree. (It wouldn't fit under the tree.) I was proud to be the one responsible for the gift looking so nice.

As the family gathered to open presents, I loudly proclaimed, "I worked really hard drawing these pictures. Whoever gets this better take their time unwrapping it. I don't want my pictures ripped up!" I failed to notice the grin, and smirk, on my brother's face.

Soon all the gifts were distributed, except for that big box. Like the night before, I again pleaded with my brother to tell me who was getting that present.

"Well, it's for you!"

The moment he spoke, I decided my crayon artwork was not worth preserving. The coaster wagon I found, after ripping through the brown paper and tearing the box open, was far more valuable.

An 80-Year Tradition...

Marching Elf | Pseudo-Elf | Running Rudolph | Thumbing Moon | Trotting Terrier | Waving Santa | Dancing Doll | Hopping Hare | Traveling Bear | Circus Seal

In 1938, Cambridge resident E. E. "Joe" Aker created an animated porch Santa Claus display for an electric company Christmas decoration contest. Children loved it, so he expanded it during the WWII years. When Joe moved away in 1968, the display was moved to the home of the late Atty. Russell Booth at 831 North Tenth Street. It continues to be maintained and run by the Booth family each year at Christmas. They hope to keep it running to at least the age of 100!

My First Job

BY BETSY TAYLOR

Sophisticated shopping.

    To be precise, I accepted my first paying job when I was thirteen. I became an afternoon-only babysitter. The job was two doors from my home and paid $.35 an hour. In case some readers might think that's not a real job, let me say babysitting is a REAL job – as real as it gets. I entered the world of business at the age of seventeen, when I went to work at Davis's Department Store.

    Davis's, on a smaller scale, could hold its own against any big city department store, even the Lazarus Company in Columbus. The windows on Wheeling Avenue were frequently re-dressed to showcase the array of goods inside. A passerby could be forgiven for thinking that Davis's was only a clothing store, but it was much more. Step inside, and it was hard to decide where to look first. A cavernous ceiling drew the eye upward. On the left, an elegant display of cosmetics and fragrances greeted customers, while on the right, stylish menswear beckoned.

    Each department was staffed with permanent employees who knew many of their customers by name, and were experts in managing merchandise. Because I worked during summers and school holidays, I was rotated through every department. That made me versatile enough to substitute wherever I was needed. My duties took me from the basement (women's bargain apparel), to the main floor (cosmetics, menswear, stationery, children's and checkout), to the second floor (women's better clothing, and infants and toddlers), and finally, to the land of dinnerware and small appliances on the top level.

During the four years I worked there, the store changed owners and became Bonham's Department Store. The name changed, but the quality of the merchandise and service remained the same. Every customer received the same degree of courtesy because, as we all knew, the customer was always right.

The Davis/Bonham Store was classy, but it was also fun, thanks to three unique features. The first, a full-size elevator, complete with an elevator operator, served customers who couldn't climb the stairs. A wide staircase enticed shoppers to a mezzanine that served as a lounge. It offered comfortable, upholstered seating and access to clean, well-equipped restrooms. The third feature, unique to Cambridge, was the checkout desk. Well-dressed salesladies and salesmen assisted shoppers in selecting their purchases, then escorted them to the desk where payment was made. A sales receipt was hand written on a pad where a carbon copy (store copy) remained. A tax table allowed the clerk to quickly add in that figure. The final cost was double checked on an adding machine and the receipt, along with the money, was rolled into a metal cylinder called a cart. (Think of the carts used at drive-through banks.) The carts were sucked into a pneumatic tube and, with a "clunk" and "whoosh," hurtled their way to the business office where change was made and the receipt was shot back to the customers. Thanks to this process, the tubes within our store's walls hummed like a maze of super highways.

By far, the most glamorous job was the buyer's position. Our buyer made trips to New York each season to scope out the hottest new fashions. But she also chose which of these styles would sell in Cambridge. Her choices were always smart and, as a result, the ladies' clothing section did a brisk business.

It was a sad time when the Davis/Bonham Department Store closed its doors. Those bygone businesses left their mark on the community. My first job allowed me to earn a minimum wage paycheck, learn a slew of skills, and introduced me to a wonderful group of people.

When Department Stores Ruled...

Above: Postcard of the Potter-Davis building, circa 1918.

Left: The Davis Department Store, circa 1955, in the same building.

Photos courtesy of the Guernsey County History Museum.

The Berwick

BY BOB LEY

Way before Holiday Inn!

In 1963, I was twenty-one and in the process of opening a business in Cambridge. Being single, I decided the easiest solution to shelter would be a hotel room rented by the month. There were three downtown choices, the Berwick Hotel being the best of them. I paid $80 per month (and was informed I could not have liquor in the room, nor entertain ladies there.)

It was run by Harry Kahn. One evening he and I sat in the lobby talking about the building's rich history. Mr. Kahn told me that Colonel Joseph Taylor, an officer in the Civil War, purchased the land in the six hundred block of Wheeling Avenue in 1866. The recently retired veteran built his first house there. He later married and built a grander home on Upland Road, several blocks north of Wheeling Avenue. That home still stands today as a beautifully restored bed and breakfast.

Colonel Taylor recognized the need for a good hotel in Cambridge, which was quickly becoming a major stop for travelers on the National Road. Even more important to travelers, the railroad ran through Cambridge beginning in 1852, further increasing the need for the hotel. He razed the Wheeling Avenue house and began construction of the hotel. The Berwick opened to great fanfare with a gala event in August of 1887. The Berwick's name was chosen because it was the name of his wife's hometown in Maine, North Berwick.

A huge fire destroyed the hotel in 1891. Taylor vowed to rebuild it and he did. The Berwick finally reopened three years later in 1894. Amazingly, another fire the next year destroyed many of the buildings Taylor had constructed around the hotel, but a firewall had spared the Berwick from further disaster.

Wheeling Avenue was paved with bricks five years later, which included brick sidewalks. New streetcar rails were added in 1902. Mr. Kahn told me the National Road viaduct bridge was damaged by the flood in 1913 and condemned. The new viaduct bridge was completed in the 1920s, soaring over Wills Creek and the railroad tracks, further enhancing the location of the Berwick Hotel.

Today the building has been repurposed into apartments for those who enjoy living in the downtown. Col. Taylor, I'm sure, would be pleased to see his building still in use these many years later.

Guernsey County can count in its history many contributors to its success. Col. Joseph Taylor was one of them.

Col. Taylor's Victorian mansion, Today's Col. Taylor Inn

Col. Joseph D. Taylor was the most prominent Cambridge citizen in the late 1800s. He served in Congress, and he built the Berwick Hotel.

Look at Your Door

BY SAMUEL D. BESKET

A bullet a day helps with your pay.

I knew when the plant manager called a meeting of all supervisors, he had something important to tell us. Rumors and speculations soared. Would we have a layoff? Was the plant shutting down? Everyone had an anxious look on their faces as Rob entered the conference room. He must have sensed this. His first words to us were to relax, he had good news. He sat on the end of the desk, his legs dangling over the side.

He got straight to the point. "Our parent company has a new CEO and he will be touring all the plants in the corporation this summer. They have us scheduled for the second week in July. As I get more details, I will pass them along to you. One thing I know about him is he doesn't like pre-planned tours. When we visit your department, ask him what he would like to see and let him decide."

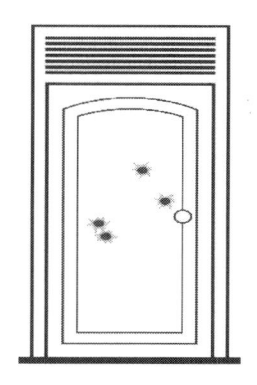

As the meeting adjourned, Rob grabbed me by the arm and said, "Hang around for a few minutes." After everyone left, he said, "Mr. Alvarez is a down-to-earth, hands on… person. He likes to mingle with the employees. I would like to start the tour in the resistor building. It's adjacent to the main plant, and our newest building. Remember, first impressions are important."

Friday, the day of the tour, dawned hot and muggy. Just as we were to start the tour, it started to rain. Rob suggested we take the company van to the resistor building to keep from getting wet. As we parked in the dock, I asked Mr. Alvarez how he wanted to proceed.

"Jose," he said. "Call me Jose. I prefer to go alone. I'll be okay, just want to walk around and talk to the people." After introducing him to everyone, I told him Rob and I would wait for him in my office.

When we returned to my office we noticed the office door was covered with fake bullet holes. Rob gave me a puzzled look, and I shrugged my shoulders. There wasn't anything we could do.

Ten minutes later, Jose came to my office, and immediately saw the bullet holes. After a pause that seemed like hours, he looked at us, rubbed his chin and said, "Interesting." My mind went blank. I had nothing. Finally, in desperation, I said, "I was late with the paychecks last Friday."

"Today is Friday," he responded immediately.

"Already paid them," was my reply.

Jose just smiled and nodded his head. As he walked to the door, he turned and said, "Smart move."

After everyone left, Jerry, my best worker and chief prankster came into my office. I suspected he was the perpetrator of the deed. After staring at the floor for a few seconds, he asked if he should wear old clothes to work on Monday.

"Why do you say that? Is there something I need to know?"

"I'll bring them Monday," Jerry said with a grin on his face.

Later that day, after everyone had left, Rob called us together to critique the visit. To our surprise, Jose had been pleased with what he had seen. It wasn't the painted floors or displays we had set up throughout the plant that impressed him. It was the attitude of the employees, how friendly they were, how they functioned as a team, and how they took ownership of their jobs.

Nothing was mentioned about the fake bullet holes on my office door. Jerry was off the hook, although I let him stew for a few days before I told him.

When Eisenhower Was President...

Champion Spark Plug started up its Cambridge plant in 1955. These photos appeared in a booklet celebrating the "All-America City" award Cambridge received that year.

Photos courtesy of the Guernsey County History Museum.

Remembering Midtown News

BY RICK BOOTH

A great place to go with Grandpa.

Mad Magazine and Matchbox cars – those were the things that made Midtown News a childhood delight for me in the 1960s. The newsstand stood in an old brick building opposite the Guernsey County Courthouse on West Eighth Street in Cambridge. Most of my earliest memories of it were of visiting the store with my grandfather when he wanted to pick up a special issue of the Columbus Dispatch or the Cleveland Plain Dealer. If I was tagging along, the trip also often meant a special treat for me as well.

In my grade school days, Matchbook cars sold for fifty cents. There were dozens of models of the tiny metal cars, only a couple of inches long. Some had a working trunk or door or hood, but all had working wheels. Thus, with Matchbox car in hand, any random board or flat surface could be slanted onto the floor to make a racetrack the likes of a Soapbox Derby. Any indoor cat or dog could be made the object of a surprise attack by a little Ford or Chevy or old-style Indy Car, too. Every few weeks a new tiny model would come out. They were collectible, of course, but I didn't obsess over getting each new offering. Grandpa was kind enough to treat me to a new car now and again, and I reciprocated, I felt, by not abusing his generosity.

It was probably about the

time I was outgrowing the Matchbox cars that I discovered the other magnificent offering of Midtown News – Mad Magazine. I suppose I could have made it through Junior High without a monthly dose of Alfred E. Neuman, but it would not have been nearly as much fun. Who can forget Spy vs. Spy? Or the movie spoofs, which were funny even though I'd rarely seen the movies they lampooned and therefore didn't always get the jokes. And then there were the fake ads that mocked Madison Avenue and probably taught my generation a thing or two about media manipulation. To the magazine's credit, their anti-cigarette mock ads likely kept thousands from adopting bad habits. Though Grandpa may have sponsored a few issues of the magazine, in time I came to visit the store alone and ration out my own meager savings for a monthly dose of humor. It was worth it!

Years later, the newsstand closed, but the name remained colorfully emblazoned on the building. It became the Courtside Deli and Midtown Bar & Grill. Then one day in December, 2015, I came across a curious old faded photo at the Guernsey County History Museum. It showed an unknown store and its employees somewhere in Cambridge about a hundred years ago. So I scanned it and computer-enhanced the detail in the picture until I came up with clues to the business name, address, and date. It was a photo of the Branthoover & Johnston store in 1902, located on West Eighth Street. Sure enough, it was the Midtown News building as it had been sixty years before my earliest memories! I immediately went out to photograph it from the same angle for comparison. Three months later, Midtown News burned down.

I'm glad I had that one last chance to snap a picture of the old building that brought back so many good memories. Someday a new building will no doubt arise there, but for me, 117 West Eighth will always be connected to a magazine called Mad, tiny cars that worked, and my generous, caring grandfather who always knew just how to make a grandson's day.

Before the Newsstand Days...

In 1902, the local plumbing firm of Branthoover & Johnston expanded its occupancy of the future Midtown News building from the right half of the building to both sides. They took this picture that fall. A window poster advertises the upcoming minstrel show of Primrose & Dockstader, coming to town on Friday, October 10th, 1902. They were to perform at the Colonial Theater opposite the Berwick Hotel.

Photo courtesy of the Guernsey County History Museum.

Gray's General Store

BY MARK COOPER

One-stop shopping before Walmart.

By the 1970s, most old-time general stores in Guernsey County had closed. But Roger and Faye Gray's store, in Birmingham, remained open to serve the community with many goods.

Benches on the building's front porch provided ample space for local men to exchange news and solve the world's problems while enjoying their chewing tobacco, pipes, and cigars. These men looked scary to me, but the rest of shopping at Gray's with my parents was a fun experience.

Inside, we could shop for everything from clothing to household supplies to fresh food. Unlike much of the clothing found in today's stores, Roger and Faye sold shirts, jeans, and shoes durable enough to stand up to the rigors of farm and country life.

Stationery supplies included notebooks, pens, pencils, erasers, and rulers. Mom purchased my one and only Big Chief writing tablet at Gray's. For years, after I'd used all the paper, I kept the tablet cover with its silhouette of the proud chief. If I still had it, I'd frame and display it in my office.

On top of the deli counter there was a massive beam scale, a large roll of brown waxed paper, and a huge spool of string. As I recall, the string ran through a couple of eyelets screwed into the ceiling, to prevent it from tangling.

Mom usually purchased Longhorn or Swiss cheese, and some kind of lunch meat. Faye weighed each selection on the scale, wrapped the food in the brown waxed paper, and tied the package securely with string. I think Mom saved every inch of that string, rolling it into little balls to stow in her kitchen cabinet until it was needed for some household project. Most likely, a little ball of that string is still buried in the dark recesses of a cabinet or kitchen drawer.

Swinging doors behind the store's deli counter separated the retail area from Roger and Faye's living quarters. I was fascinated that their store was also their home and kept trying to catch glimpses of Faye's kitchen beyond those doors.

Gray's inventory included farm boots and tires kept in a barn next to the store. I felt very grown up the day Roger took me up to the barn to fit me with a pair of gum boots. Besides making sure us country folk got the boots we needed for tromping through farm mud and muck, Roger also repaired old tires or sold new ones to area drivers.

Each time we shopped at Gray's, Mom allowed me to pick out a snack. Cracker Jacks were a favorite, since each box concealed a treasure that could be anything from a tiny pinball game to a miniscule sketch pad. Another treat I enjoyed was orange sherbet pop-ups. After finishing the sherbet, I'd pretend the plastic "pop-up" was an umbrella. That two-inch plastic disc certainly would not have offered much protection in an actual rainstorm.

A great-uncle once gave me a dollar and instructed me to buy myself an all-day sucker. I found that the sucker's value was in its size rather than in its taste.

Once, when I had a loose tooth, Gray's provided me with dental care. Mom had bought me a taffy Sugar Daddy. After only a few licks, I looked down and saw my tooth firmly embedded in the sticky sucker. That was a much sweeter way to get a tooth pulled than going to the dentist.

For forty years, Roger and Faye served the community well with their store. Today, it and other general stores like theirs are long gone. But the memories of those shopping experiences remain rich. And free.

A Long Time Ago...

Ellwood's General Store was located on the west side of Highland Avenue, near where today's Health Department office is located, but on the opposite side of the street. The Red Crown Gasoline advertised in the sign at right was produced by the Standard Oil Company of Indiana, today's Amoco.

Photo courtesy of the Guernsey County History Museum, Adair Collection.

Sidewalk Sales in Cambridge

BY MARK COOPER

When even the guys enjoyed shopping!

Before the days of shopping centers, chain discount stores, and on-line shopping, Cambridge offered its annual sidewalk sales. Savvy shoppers made plans to stock up on regularly used items, as well as a luxury item or two that would be above budget any other time.

Prior to the sale, The Jeffersonian was full of enticing ads promising great savings on merchandise. Once the sale days arrived, throngs of people crowded downtown, creating a festive atmosphere.

As I recall, the sidewalk sale took place on the third weekend of each July. For many years, that weekend corresponded with the hottest days of summer. But the heat did not discourage bargain seekers.

Sidewalks along both sides of Wheeling Avenue were jammed with shelves, racks, and bins placed outside of each store, to display discounted wares. J.C. Penney's and Robert's Men Shop featured clothing. Both Gallenkamp and Alexander Shoe Stores offered racks of shoes, and probably a shade or two of shoe polish. Kresge's provided lots of browsing fun, with reduced prices on items ranging from toys to household goods. Even the pharmacy offered a sale table of personal care products.

Moving along the sidewalk was never a speedy

journey, as eager shoppers jockeyed for position at the bargain table or rack of their choice. The action was all outside that weekend. If a person did need to slip inside a store for some reason, they would find it almost empty of other customers.

Of course, the weather wasn't always cooperative. July's intense summer heat might produce intermittent rain showers. When that happened, clerks grabbed sheets of plastic to throw over and protect their goods until the rain stopped. Once in a while, the entire weekend was stormy, forcing each retailer to set up the sale tables in their stores, rather than on the sidewalk. For some reason, the excitement of the bargain hunt was never as enjoyable inside.

A few years ago, I was at a mall and saw a sign advertising their indoor sidewalk sale. Looking forward to reliving my childhood experience, I hurried inside. Discounted merchandise was set up in the spacious concourse. No threat of rain or storm could dampen the event. Nor did shoppers experience sweltering temperatures, as central air conditioning provided comfortable temperatures.

But neither was the excitement present. Only a few stores were participating in the sale, and their displays seemed sparse. There were no crowds of people jostling against one another. There was no thrill of the hunt for the perfect bargain.

Although the mall's sidewalk sale eliminated inconveniences, it also lacked the energy and enthusiasm of the sales I remembered. Cambridge's sidewalk sales were the real deal.

Chicken Feed

BY BEVERLY WENCEK KERR

Get the Mash! Get the chicken mash!

Long ago during my childhood, one Saturday stop every week involved Thompson Feeds on 2nd Street in Cambridge. When you have thousands of chickens, a stop for chicken feed ranks high on the list of importance.

This weekly adventure required careful preparations. They all began in May, when Dad planted the field of corn, and continued until late September when Mom harvested it. In the fall, Mom spent her day in the corn field while Dad worked at Cambridge Glass and I attended Hopewell School.

All day she filled burlap bags with corn, leaving the bags in the field for Dad to pick up when he came home from work. That evening he would load the bags in the pickup, dump them in our corncrib and have empty bags for her to fill the next day.

After the corn was picked and dried in the wooden corncrib, which had cracks to let the air through, we spent our evenings at the corn sheller. At first we used a hand-crank sheller that took the grains right off the ears. Later, Dad got an electric sheller, which made things much faster.

Once shelled, we loaded up a few bags for Thompson Feeds. We basically traded shelled corn for chicken feed. Sometimes our own corn might have been used in the feed we purchased, but just as likely not.

Mom always wanted to stop at the feed mill because

the chicken feed came in pretty patterned bags. She tried to get enough of the same pattern to make kitchen curtains, matching pillowcases, or perhaps even a skirt for me. It amazes me now, how Mom could make a use for just about anything and everything.

Saturday trips to town also served another purpose. Early on Saturday morning before going to town, Mom would butcher about twenty chickens to deliver to people on our egg route. She prepared the eggs on Friday. Where did she get all her energy?

Her day of rest happened on Sunday, when she taught Sunday School at Hopewell Methodist Church. But before she went, she prepared everything she could ahead of time so she could invite the minister for, yes, you guessed it...a chicken dinner on a beautiful tablecloth made of Thompson Feed sacks!

Can You Spot the Author?...

The Hopewell School students at Indian Camp, April 17, 1952.

Fired from My First Job

BY MARTHA F. JAMAIL

A penny saved is not necessarily a penny earned.

My parents believed children should work as soon as they were of age, so when I became 16, Mom informed me I would be going to work that summer. Actually I was very excited about it.

Mother worked downtown managing a ladies clothing store, so she knew many of the shopkeepers on Yazoo Avenue, the main street in Clarksdale, Mississippi. The lady she had spoken with was Sally Landou, who owned the Gift and Art Shop. Her shop was well-known for all the lovely items displayed there, from ladies' accessories and artworks, to fine china and silver. It was also where many couples signed up to register their choice of wedding gifts, so she had plans for a busy summer and seemed as anxious as I was to get started.

Prior to my first day on the job, Mrs. Landou had me come in after hours to help price items for the next day's sale. My job was to retag all the sets of earrings for the sale table marked – "All Earrings – $1.00 a pair." She had laid out a large box of earrings for me to price, as well as additional earrings already marked $2.00 and others marked 50 cents. Many of the earrings were already marked $1.00, but the 50 cent sets greatly outnumbered the $2.00 sets. Anyway, I dutifully changed prices so that all earrings were clearly marked $1.00 a pair.

The next morning I showed up early, and Mrs. Landou put me to work at the front counter. About mid-morning, an elderly African-American woman walked in and I greeted her. She smiled, nodding, and seeing the $1.00 earring table, she walked over to browse through the choices. It wasn't long before she chose a pair of yellow floral dangly earrings. I remember noticing them too, the day before, and their 50-cent price tag.

As she approached the counter, she placed the earrings there and, digging through her pockets, pulled out a white knotted handkerchief. I watched as her gnarled fingers slowly worked to loosen the knot, and finally she removed the coins – two quarters. She checked her other pockets, then apologized for not having enough money. When she turned to replace the earrings on the sale table, I stopped her and said, "No, that's okay. Your two quarters will be enough." I made the entry and rang up the sale, thinking the earrings were only 50 cents anyway.

After she left, Mrs. Landou approached me and in a scolding tone said, "Honey, I saw what just happened. I run a business here and you shouldn't have done that. I have to make a profit."

"I know, Mrs. Landou," I replied, "but they were 50 cent earrings anyway, and that was all the money she had."

"Now, Martha, if that's the way you feel, I guess you can't work for me. I'm sorry, but I have to let you go."

"Okay," I said quietly, then got my purse and walked out the door and across the street to the shop where my mother worked.

Mother looked

questioningly at me when I walked through the door, and I told her what had happened. She just shook her head slowly and said she would talk to Mrs. Landou after closing. I walked home despondently, regretting what I had done.

At the end of the workday, Mom arrived home, all smiles, and said she and Sally had come to an agreement. I could return to work the next day, but I would not be working the front counter. My new job would be to inventory all items in the stockroom, including all deliveries, and arrange them on the display shelves. I really enjoyed my new job, because I got a preview of many lovely sets of china, and chose the set I still use today.

Readers, be wary when shopping a store that has a special sale table. You just might be paying more than the item originally cost.

When a Dollar Went Far...

There were once several neighborhood A&P stores in Cambridge. Nothing in this one's display window was priced above 39 cents.

Photo courtesy of the Guernsey County History Museum, Adair Collection.

A Fun Place

BY BOB LEY

Wooden ya know!

Driving down Woodlawn Avenue by the empty field that used to be Cambridge Lumber always leaves me with good memories. It was owned and run by John and Walter Fairchild. One of my favorite pastimes was woodworking. I loved building furniture, did considerable remodeling, even built a wooden speedboat. I spent numerous happy hours at Cambridge Lumber.

At the time, there was no other place around that offered the selection of quality tools and lumber, as well as services usually found only in bigger cities. Every trip to Cambridge Lumber was tantamount to receiving the Sears catalog. Power tools, most of which were beyond my financial reach then, but worth dreaming about, were available with knowledgeable people willing to explain how they worked.

A fully-equipped woodworking shop occupied part of the building. Skilled cabinetmakers could duplicate anything needed that could not be done with a typical homeowner's tools. No project I ever had done by the woodworking shop seemed to faze them.

Inside the main building was an office occupied by Walter Guegold, their Design Engineer. He designed building projects from dog houses, decks, and gazebos to homes and commercial buildings. He furnished a list showing the products, sizes, and quantity needed, estimating the cost to complete the project. Walter did a room addition for me and it was a very professional job.

John and Walter Fairchild ran a wonderful business, but as with many small businesses, the big box stores, though some distance away, began to take their toll. Interstate highways have allowed customers to easily swap caring, personal service for volume and even larger selections.

I really miss it!

When They Harvested Trees...

Kimbolton was once home to the Gregg lumber yard. It was located on the south side of the village. This picture, sent on a 1917 postcard, shows only a fraction of the lumber yard's size. Later that year, the United States entered the First World War.

Photo courtesy of the Guernsey County History Museum.

Full Circle

BY SAMUEL D. BESKET

It just keeps floating along.

The sound of an airplane flying overhead sent my brother and me flying out the back door. Sure enough, a shiny yellow airplane was making its final approach to Lore City Airport. This scenario repeated itself many times on summer days, when small planes made regular flights in and out of our small grass airport.

In our haste to get outside, we forgot the screen door was hooked to keep my younger brother in the house. How many times Dad replaced the hook on the storm door is still a mystery today. As I grew older, my interest in flying continued to grow, and still does.

The Lore City Flying Service was a small airport with a 2,000-foot grass landing strip. It was established in the late 40s and flourished until the 70s. Many a young man learned to fly at this small grass field.

Sunday afternoons were prime time for flying. We would walk to the airport with my father to watch the planes take off and land. We yearned for a ride, but Dad wasn't sold on the safety of the small canvas-covered planes.

A few years later, our dreams came true when we were given a free ride in a silver 180 Cessna. This plane was all metal, had seats for four, and a radio for communications. This was a drastic change from the smaller canvas planes we were used to seeing. The fellow that owned the plane must have sensed our enthusiasm for flying, because he went to great lengths to explain how the airplane functioned.

Years later, after serving in the Air Force, I returned home only to see a shiny yellow airplane sitting in front of the old airport hangar. Curiosity got the best of me, and I walked over to see it. To my surprise, it was owned by someone I knew, who was restoring it. I offered to help, and he accepted. Once again, a shiny yellow airplane was back in my life.

After months of testing, we finally flew the plane. Over the next few years, we spent many warm summer days floating over the hills of Guernsey and Noble Counties. It was fun flying over the interstate highway and watching the cars pass under us. Their speed was faster than ours, but we had a much better view.

Now, fifty years removed, our home is located in the landing pattern for Cambridge Airport. I still have a hankering to run outside every time I hear a plane coming in for a landing. The fascination is still there.

Every September, there is a fly-in at Cambridge Airport. It's a fun day, with dozens of airplanes from all eras on display. On one particular day, I noticed a shiny yellow airplane parked on the tarmac. After talking to the owner, I realized it was the same plane I flew in fifty years ago. Incidentally, he was the nephew of the original owner.

"The Piper Cub is the safest plane in the world. It can just barely kill you."

– Max Stanley, test pilot

Aunt Ruth's Store

BY BETSY TAYLOR

The neighborhood grocery.

From the age of four, I lived on Stewart Avenue in Cambridge. At the west end of our block, my aunt and uncle operated a small mom-'n-pop grocery store. During the fifties and early sixties, thirty-two of those small stores dotted the city. Most people in the community had never shopped in a supermarket. In fact, there were no "super" markets, just bigger grocery stores. A&P and Kroger were the larger food markets, along with the M&K Market on South 10th Street.

If you needed a carton of eggs, a loaf of bread, or a can of green beans, a quick walk to a small, local store, satisfied those needs. Since there were no plastic bags, and paper bags didn't have handles, shoppers hiked home hugging a bag of groceries.

Aunt Ruth's store was really named Cain's Neighborhood Grocery. The store occupied the first floor of an old two-story gray house close to the corner of Stewart Avenue and 7th Street.

I was seven years old when I went to "work" at Aunt Ruth's store. After school, I hung out stocking the lowest shelves, sweeping dust around the creaky wood floors, and keeping Aunt Ruth entertained as she supervised my homework. My pay took the form of penny candy, a popsicle, or an occasional dime.

Smoking was usual during the fifties, and kids could be sent to buy tobacco with no questions asked. I remember experimenting with division before I knew what it was. There are 20 cigarettes in a package at a cost of 21 cents. How much does each cigarette cost? I admit, I couldn't figure out the part about the left-over penny.

While in the store, I had the chance to watch adults interact. I rarely saw adults in my family talk with anyone outside the family. They did all that at their own jobs. But here, I could observe grown-ups politely dealing with each other. Sometimes it was all business and sometimes it was chatty small talk as shoppers browsed. I noticed that many of Aunt Ruth's customers were elderly ladies who didn't drive, and many lived alone.

My cool after-school hangout spot disappeared when Aunt Ruth became a nurse's aide at Guernsey Memorial Hospital, and closed the business. I recall that her store was never very busy. Nevertheless, there were many neighbors who missed the place for a while. Fortunately, Harold's Royal Blue Market in the 400 block of 8th Street, was down the street and just around the corner. That store absorbed her customers quickly. As an endorsement, Aunt Ruth shopped there regularly praising their service, selection, and quality of their products.

Today, shoppers have choices of a plethora of food brands in super-duper mega-marts, along with a variety of non-food products under the same roof. One-stop shopping has replaced individual trips to a grocery store, hardware store, book store, paint store, stationery store, clothing store, or sporting goods store. Convenience has replaced getting to know vendors who personalized the shopping experience. For my money, we have lost a lot to big box stores.

Can we manage a turnaround? Villages seem to have the best chance, but it looks like the ship that carried Aunt Ruth's store has sailed.

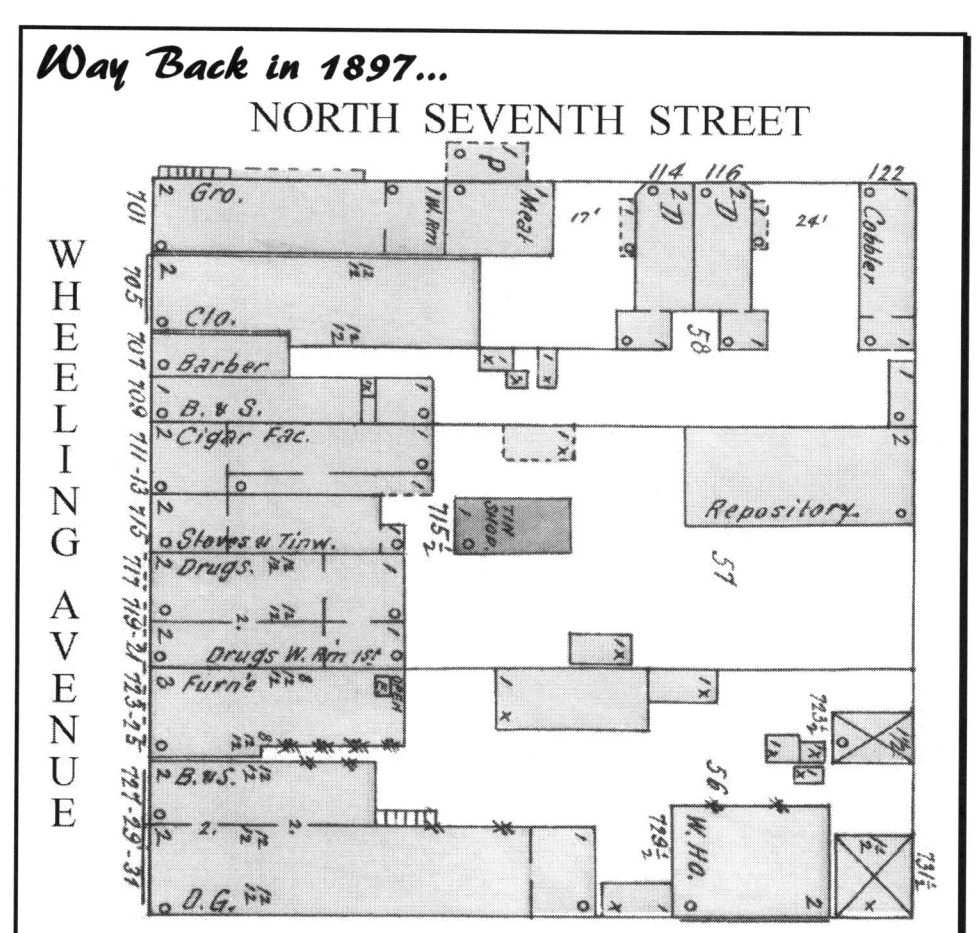

Way Back in 1897...
NORTH SEVENTH STREET

Cambridge was once full of small stores. In 1897, in just one quarter of a city block, an old map shows a grocer, a clothier, a barber, a boot and shoe store, a cigar factory, stoves and tinware, a drug store, a furniture store, more boots and shoes, dry goods, a meat market, a cobbler, and two horse stables (buildings with a big "X" on top).

Don't Lose Your Marbles

BY BETSY TAYLOR

Big industry in a small city.

Today, Cambridge, Ohio, is a thriving city that, during its rich history, supported a multitude of diverse industries. Buggy whips, huge blocks of ice, and electronic components are examples of practical products manufactured here. Cambridge also holds a respected place in catalogs of artistic creations that are, nationally and internationally, collectibles of great value.

One such collectible is marbles – the common, roll-around-in-the-dirt-on-the-playground variety. In 1927, the A.G. Christensen Marble Company (also called Christensen Agate) set up a manufacturing plant beside the Cambridge Glass Company in East Cambridge. Today, the Guernsey County maintenance garage sits in its place. The rationale for the location was based on an agreement with Cambridge Glass that granted Christensen Agate permission to harvest and recycle the glass company's salvaged glass as raw material. Natural gas to fuel the plant's operations was plentiful in the area as well. However, Cambridge was also a great manufacturing site because of the historic National Road that runs through the city's downtown. Even in 1927, the road was the nation's busiest highway.

In its heyday, the marble

company turned out an astounding 300,000 marbles a day, and developed a reputation for producing the "most perfectly formed marbles in the nation." Since every boy, and many girls, wanted a bag of marbles, the pool of customers was enormous.

One innovation that advanced Christensen Agate was M.F. Christensen's invention of a machine that made perfectly round marbles. The machine fed a stream of melted glass from the furnace through a small hole. A spinning blade cut off the precise length of gooey glass needed to make a marble. This glob of glass entered a rotating chamber, where it was rolled, as if you rolled a lump of clay between your palms, to make a perfect, round ball. The marble cooled as it rolled down a tube and fell into a bucket, where it was hand gathered. Not only did the machine make a more perfect product, it also made marbles cheaper to produce.

Exquisite pigments were added to the molten glass. Because of their brightness, the resulting colors were called electric colors. In today's market, some colors are more desirable, as are some designs. Websites that promote purchases, sales, and swaps of Christensen marbles are plentiful. I've discovered a whole "marble culture" out there.

In 1933, the Christensen Agate Company closed its doors. While in business, it didn't employ many workers and didn't have a huge influence on the local economy. But today, a Cambridge, Ohio, product carries a worldwide stellar reputation for high quality and artistic excellence. If you own any of these perfect marbles, guard them well.

They are priceless.

Goblets Fit for a King...

The Cambridge Glass Company sought and received over 100 patents for its products and designs between 1903 and 1949. This 1930 goblet design was credited to Wilbur L. Orme.

Sandman

BY BEVERLY WENCEK KERR

Living his dream.

Breaker, Breaker. This is Sandman. Has anybody got their ears on?

Dad kept his CB in the big building behind our house. There he could talk without interruptions and meet people all around the area. Since Dad enjoyed traveling, this provided a way to escape life in Guernsey County.

His grandson wondered, "Why do you call yourself Sandman?"

"You know I've worked at making glass all my life," answered Gramps. For forty-five years he had worked at Cambridge Glass Company. When it closed, Dad (Rudy Wencek), Tom Mosser, and Mary Martha Mitchell owned their own glass company, Variety Glass. Glass making was of great importance to him, and the world he knew best.

"But what's that got to do with a sandman? I thought they helped put you to sleep by putting sand in your eyes. That's what Mom told me."

"Well," chuckled Gramps, "I'm not that kind of a sandman."

Then he went on to explain how glass was made from sand, an intricate part of the process, with lime and soda added. Glass is actually made from liquid sand. You can melt ordinary sand into liquid sand at extremely high temperatures, but the quality of the sand is of utmost importance.

Both Cambridge Glass and Variety Glass purchased their silica sand from Pennsylvania and Michigan.

Fine white silica sand is used as a base in all types of specialty glass and does not contain any other chemicals. This makes the best clear glass. Other ingredients must be added for colored glass.

Making glass isn't a new idea, as the Egyptians made colored glass beads for jewelry over 3000 years ago. Way back in 1851, a house made of glass, the Crystal Palace, was built for the Great Exhibition. Glass has been around for a long time and still remains quite popular.

"Throughout my years in the glass industry, I've been everything from a carrying-in boy to a presser and glass blower. Once, when the furnaces were down, they sent me to the etching room, but shortly told me never to return there again." Gramps shook his head and smiled as he remembered his experience there.

"In the etching department, they told me I would be the printer and rub the design on etching paper from a metal plate. Think my fingers were just too big as I never seemed to get the entire design on the etching paper. The ladies in the department really gave me a hard time. If the etching wasn't copied perfectly, the entire piece of glass had to be thrown away."

"Did you know it took seventy people to make some of those pretty pieces of glassware back when I worked at Cambridge Glass? We never realized we were making things people would collect and save all their lives."

"Wow, Gramps!" exclaimed the grandson. "I had no idea how much work went into making a piece of glass. Now I see why you like to be called Sandman."

While the Sandman has gone to that great Glass Castle in the heavens, memories of him live on in our lives each day. The grandsons never forget his stories. A crystal paperweight he made for me sits on my piano as a daily reminder of the best Sandman ever.

ॐRDW ॐ

In the Heyday of Glass...

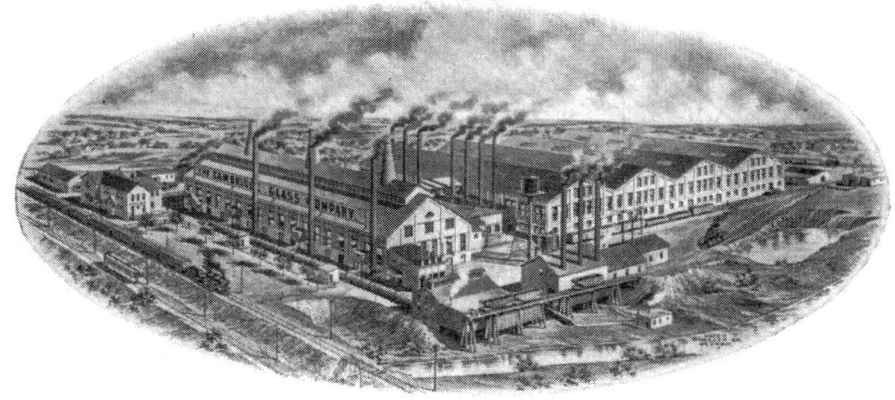

Postcard and bird's-eye view of the Cambridge Glass Company factory, circa 1910. Its employees went on to found a number of other local glass companies, including Variety Glass and today's Mosser Glass, the last operating Cambridge Glass Company descendant.

Photos courtesy of the Guernsey County History Museum.

A Guys' World

BY JOY L. WILBERT ERSKINE

A very hairy situation.

It was a typical hometown barber shop, at least in my uneducated estimation. I'd never been in one before. Two barber chairs; a wall of mirrors and cabinetry; a rack full of fishing, hunting, sports, and news magazines. The barber's wife must have decorated the small room—a baseball-themed wallpaper border circled the room above dark half-paneling. A framed caricature of Jerry, the lone barber, depicted as a baseball player, was displayed prominently on one wall—probably a good conversation starter for a topic he loved to talk about.

Utilitarian chairs lined two walls, practically all filled, mostly with retirees, but also with working men with an hour to get a haircut before reporting to work nearby. A couple of bored-looking teenagers, long legs sprawling into the middle of the room, awaited their turns. One cute little sprout had come with his dad for his first haircut, a guys' world, definitely. Some of the fellows were obviously regulars, just there to chew the fat with Jerry and the other men, passing the time until heading home for dinner. But most were waiting for haircuts, joining in on the topic of the day. The barber was unrushed. He took his time with every customer and kept the conversation lively. It was a popular place.

When I pushed through the door and asked if women could get haircuts there, all conversation stopped;

magazines dropped below eye level; every ear tuned in, awaiting the answer. A guy returned from the men's room, confused at the silence until he saw me. He quickly, sheepishly, found a seat. Explaining that a short haircut was virtually impossible to get at the local beauty salons, I repeated my question and waited for Jerry's response.

Jerry was a small, trim man who wore a perpetual smile across his angular face. He paused, scissors hovering over the head of an elderly man, and beamed at me. "Well, of course you can, Ma'am. Have a seat! I'll be with you in a few minutes." The lull in conversation slowly dissipated as I quietly settled into my seat. Soon, the men were heatedly engaged in local politics and before long the language got a little crusty. I buried my nose in a Newsweek magazine, trying to ignore it. Jerry noticed. He commanded attention with a low grunt, a "look," and a discreet nod in my direction. The conversation cleaned up instantly.

It was the beginning of a long, friendly relationship. My turn in the chair came and Jerry took his time, giving me the full benefit of his years teaching barbering and cutting hair. He was a classy guy who knew his business.

He retired a number of years back, and moved to Florida. I'm not sure I've forgiven him. I haven't had as good a haircut since.

Erven and Rowland
Cambridge's Exclusive Barber Shop

A CLEAN STEAM TOWEL WITH EVERY SHAVE

826 Wheeling Ave. Phone 2388
Beauty Shop, Phone 2570

This barber shop ad was found in a 1930 Colonial Theater program.

Memories of 7819 Railroad Avenue

BY JOY L. WILBERT ERSKINE

A good kind of Southern California tremor.

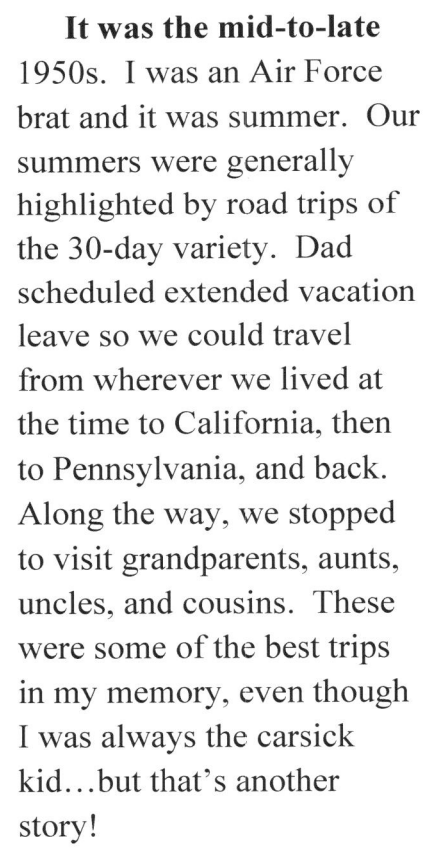

It was the mid-to-late 1950s. I was an Air Force brat and it was summer. Our summers were generally highlighted by road trips of the 30-day variety. Dad scheduled extended vacation leave so we could travel from wherever we lived at the time to California, then to Pennsylvania, and back. Along the way, we stopped to visit grandparents, aunts, uncles, and cousins. These were some of the best trips in my memory, even though I was always the carsick kid…but that's another story!

Grandma and Grandpa White lived in Riverside, California, at 7819 Railroad Avenue, named for, yes, the railroad tracks that ran long their road…several sets of tracks, to be exact. Railroad Avenue was a dusty dirt street back then, lined on the track side with citrus and nut packing plants that used the railroad to distribute their goods. Grandma packed grapefruits, oranges, and walnuts. Grandpa worked at the steel mill and grew lemons, avocados, grapes, and other fruit-bearing trees and plants in the backyard.

When I think of those times, it's always in the context of the trains across the street. Life at Grandma and Grandpa's house was punctuated throughout the day and night by the rumble of steel wheels on the tracks and the shrill whistle of locomotives. I can still smell the coffee Grandma brewed for Grandpa early every morning; hear their comforting, quiet small talk in the kitchen before the household woke up; and feel the sweet, cool air as I washed dishes under the kitchen window after dinner at night.

There was a rhythm to life by the rails that I've experienced nowhere else. I remember running to the front door to watch whenever an engine screeched along the tracks, hauling endless lines of lumbering boxcars behind them. I always imagined where they might be going, what it would be like to travel with them. It was somehow comforting to lie listening to the trains late at night, feeling the house shudder, giggling at the way the vibrations chattered my teeth. Stories of hoboes riding the rails raced through my head. I dreamed what it would be like to do that myself, and often wondered what we would do if a real tramp knocked on Grandma's door looking for a meal.

When it was time to fix dinner, we moved the kitchen table to climb down the hatch in the floor to retrieve Grandma's home-canned meats, vegetables, and fruits. It was quieter down there. When the trains passed by, you could hear the jars tinkle together and watch the juices dance inside the bottles. Sometimes, a jar of green beans or applesauce would vibrate right off the shelf, dropping to a shattering demise on the stone floor. Grandma was never happy about that.

In the afternoon, it was a treat to watch cartoons on Grandpa's television because we still had no TV at our own home in those early years. We often strained to hear the television as yet another engine barreled noisily through the neighborhood. Dad and Grandpa watched the evening news with Chet Huntley and David Brinkley live from New York and Washington, D.C., and discussed it thoroughly – sometimes as Mom and Grandma hurriedly pushed us kids out the kitchen door into the backyard, out of hearing. If we'd been allowed to stay, I'm sure we would have learned some really fascinating things.

Railroad Avenue has changed over the years. The house at 7819 was torn down somewhere along the way, replaced by a more modern one. The railroad tracks have multiplied but, surprisingly, the packing house where Grandma used to work is still standing. The dirt road is paved now, but as I google satellite photos of the old neighborhood, it's not so different that I can't picture in my mind the way it used to be. I still feel the rhythm of the rails rumble to life again, if only in my heart. After all, that's where it's always been.

On the Year of Custer's Last Stand...

This train was caught heading north toward Newcomerstown along North Third Street in Cambridge in an 1876 panoramic photo. This north-south line, known as the Cleveland and Marietta Railroad, later became part of the Pennsylvania Railroad system. It actually ran from Marietta to Dover, though it originally had aspired to run as far as Cleveland and was named accordingly.

The Telegrapher and the Comet

BY RICK BOOTH

Waiting for Halley's return.

There were two stories my grandfather told repeatedly when reminiscing about his youth: the first, of seeing a comet in 1910, and the second, of his work as a railroad telegrapher. They told of pride and premonition.

Grandpa was born in 1899 in his family's old log house on a farm that is now part of Salt Fork State Park. On a clear night, with no electric lights in the area, the heavens he saw were resplendent. His fondest memory of that sky was of seeing Halley's Comet in 1910. Night after night, he would lay on a hillside watching the great comet streak toward the sun as its tail whipped at Earth. Besides the comet's sky-spanning beauty, what intrigued him most was the thought that the splendid sky-beast would be back again in 76 years for his grandchildren to see.

My grandfather began wistfully telling me his story of the comet in the early 1960s. He spoke of it with awe, but always ended the tale with the poignant statement that I would see the comet in my lifetime, but he would not again see it in his. The story always ended with that poignant bit of sting. I'd always say I hoped he was wrong, that he might live until 1986. "No, I won't," he'd reply, "but you will."

The other story I so

frequently heard was of his having become one of the youngest telegraphers working for the Pennsylvania Railroad. He grew up near the little town of Tyner, a few miles north of Cambridge, and watched the telegraphers practicing their trade at the tiny station there. He learned to decipher the tapping sounds they made. Then he practiced Morse code with them. At age 19, he was deemed fluent enough to be hired as one of the regular station telegraphers. That a huge railroad trusted its trains to a teenage farm boy like him seemed such a great honor! With pride, he took on the heavy responsibility of handling the messages that controlled the trains. He pondered the weighty thought that his skill with a telegraph key was all that kept engines, engineers, and their passengers safe from collision. A mistake could be deadly.

Grandpa's telegraphy skills subsequently landed him a job with AT&T. In later years, as the need for telegraphers disappeared, he instead worked a company diagnostic switchboard, troubleshooting phone lines. In his nearly 40 years with AT&T, he only missed two days of work before his retirement in 1964. He was proud of that, too.

In 1981, while I was living just outside New York City, I got the sad call that Grandpa had died of a sudden heart attack. I thought then of his prediction about the comet. Grandpa was right; he would not see its return.

In 1986, I was still living near New York when Halley's Comet came by again. But this time, the stars aligned badly for seeing it. It was passing by on nearly the opposite side of the sun. Best viewing was shortly after sunset, and even then, it was said to be little more than a small, hairy-looking smudge. From light-polluted New York City, it was nearly impossible to make the comet out. In fact, I never could see it from there.

The thought crossed my mind that by driving fifty or a hundred miles away, I could likely see old Halley on a clear night, as my grandfather had predicted I would. But the comet would be dim, small, and distant – a mere shadow of its former self. Reflecting on Halley's paltry present showing, contrasted with my grandfather's long-ago vision and dreams, I saw no need for the trip. Grandpa was wrong. I would not see the comet in my lifetime. I had seen it in his.

Not Exactly a Mansion...

Playacting a holdup at the Tyner telegraphy station, circa 1915.
Photo courtesy of the Guernsey County History Museum, Adair Collection.

The Land of Hope

BY BEVERLY WENCEK KERR

America the Beautiful.

America! Many residents of foreign countries in the early 1900s looked to this land as their place of hope. My grandparents were among those immigrants. Grandfather, who we called Dede, came here to find a job working in the coal mines. Several of his family had settled in the Byesville area, so it seemed only natural that he would settle there too.

Dede, known to friends as George Veselenak, considered himself lucky to have a job at the Ideal Coal Mine. Over 400 men were employed at this large mine, which was the most productive in Guernsey County, with a vein of coal over five feet thick.

With this thick vein, it was easier to load your coal cars and get the mere ten cents a ton for each car loaded with good coal. But it was better than being hungry and these immigrants did not speak good English, so had to work where they could find a job.

Records had to be kept and most of the immigrants were illiterate. Since Dede could read and write, he most likely had a job at the coal mine in the tipple, where they weighed the coal.

Unfortunately, that left our grandmother, Baba, at home with the children. Baba was a great mother but she had one weakness. Storms! She would shudder and hide when a storm came through. Makes you wonder if perhaps she experienced some terrible storms on their boat ride over to America.

Dede knew how scared she was. When he heard that a storm was coming, he would head home from the Ideal Coal Mine over the 10th Street bridge in Byesville to comfort her.

Working in the mine didn't last long for Dede. Perhaps he was let go for running home to be with Baba, or maybe he decided he would provide a place for people to get food away from the company store.

Veselenak's Grocery appeared on 9th Street in Byesville in 1919. As you can tell from his care and concern for Baba, it's no surprise that he cared about people in general. No one was going to go hungry where he lived in The Bottom, the area on the south side of the railroad tracks.

Trading was a popular way of getting needed supplies. If you brought in eggs from your chickens, you could go home with needed flour or sugar. Or you might trade fresh vegetables in the summertime for a piece of bacon.

Even if you didn't have something to trade, Dede kept track of every purchase on his books, which we still have today. You can see where people paid him when they had the money, and he deducted it from their total. Many bills were never paid.

While working in the coal mine brought him to this country, having his own grocery store would have been a pleasant experience after work at the mines. But with eight children, it was always a difficult life. One thing for sure, they didn't go hungry.

Here It Comes

BY SAMUEL D. BESKET

A tale of three boys and a penny.

The haunting shrill of the train whistle as it passed Gibson Station was a signal that it was a few miles away. Three young boys crouched in the bushes beside the tracks, waiting its arrival. Occasionally, one of my buddies would run to the tracks and put his ear to the rail.

"Getting close," he would shout. "I can hear the clicky-clack of its wheels beating on the rail joints."

Three copper pennies lay equally spaced on the rails. As the train drew near, the coins would vibrate, almost dance, before being flattened by the giant black monster.

Finally, the engine rounded Chester's Curve, steam gushed from the drive cylinders while black smoke poured from the stack. Just as quickly as it came, it was gone, leaving us in a swirl of dust and coal smoke. A short distance down the tracks, we heard the explosion of the two torpedoes left by the preceding train to signal its departure.

As the train neared Lore City, the red signals on the crossing guard would start to blink and Mr. Davies, the telegrapher, would emerge from his office with a long-handled fork in his hand. Standing straight and close to the tracks, he would hold the fork high in the air, with a note attached to a string between the fork tines.

The train engineer hung from his cab with his left arm extended, and snagged the string with the attached note. A few seconds later, he would throw the string away and speed on toward Cambridge. When everything was clear and Mr. Davies went back to his office, we would retrieve our flattened pennies. On the way home, we would look for the lead straps used to attach the torpedoes to the rails. They made excellent sinkers for our fishing poles.

Sunday afternoons were the safest time to walk the tracks, because few trains ran on weekends. We spent many afternoons walking with Dad. He stressed why we should only walk on the side tracks, not the main line, and always be alert for trains. Occasionally, he would stop, look, and listen. He would repeat this many times, stressing to us to be alert for approaching trains. I suspect he knew we would be on the tracks going fishing and wanted us to be safe. After all, as a young boy, he had walked the same tracks years ago.

In the Age of Steam...

Westbound train emerging from Tunnel Hill tunnel at Cambridge.
Photo courtesy of the Guernsey County History Museum, Adair Collection.

Name Badges

BY BOB LEY

An ID for riding the rails!

My brother and I spent six to eight weeks with my grandparents every summer, and we got there by train. On my first trip, I was six and my brother, John, was four. (Can you imagine letting your children do that today?)

The Baltimore and Ohio ran a passenger train from Parkersburg to Cumberland, Maryland. Perhaps it went farther than that, but my grandparents lived in Maryland and we lived in Parkersburg, so that's the only stretch I know for sure.

Sitting on the big wooden benches in the station, we waited for the train. The excitement of the trip dimmed a little when Mom brought out two name badges with our names, our parents' names, and our phone number printed on them. I felt that if I was old enough to ride a train for six hours and watch a four-year-old, I didn't need a *child's* badge!

My complaint never got out. I heard the train before it could be seen. With its approach the station burst into activity. Carts, filled with suitcases pushed by baggage handlers, clackety-clacked to the platform. Passengers sitting around us, almost comatose before, leaped to life.

The train whizzed by in a cloud of steam and dust. Papers flew. Brakes whistled and screamed. The train finally came to a halt, disgorging a few passengers. Mom checked to be sure I had our tickets. Dad talked to the conductor, a tall black man in a black suit, wearing a conductor's cap. He looked over at us, flashing a big smile. I found out later Dad had tipped him to keep an eye on us and get us off at Cumberland, Maryland.

We kissed Mom and Dad and boarded the train. The conductor came by and punched our tickets. He winked at us and asked if we needed anything. "Do we have to wear these stupid name badges?" I asked.

"Not until we get close to Cumberland," he chuckled. "You guys have grown so much your grandparents might not know you." Satisfied with that logic, we snapped off the badges and sat back to watch the scenery. It was a great trip.

End of an Era...

Passengers await the last train out of Cambridge, 1961.
Photo courtesy of the Guernsey County History Museum, Adair Collection.

The Blizzard of '78

BY BETSY TAYLOR

A white hurricane!

On the morning of January 25, 1978, I awoke on my living room sofa. My husband stirred around upstairs getting ready for work. He made my breakfast, made sure I was comfortable, had all the reading material an invalid would need, kissed me, and left for his teaching job. "Sleep," he ordered as he closed the front door.

"I don't need sleep," I grumbled. "The doctor said, 'rest', not sleep. I can rest with my eyes open." Medical orders included that I not climb stairs and lift nothing heavier than a rolled-up newspaper following recent major surgery. Walking around my house in moderation was encouraged. I could even walk across the room and turn on the TV…if I wanted to.

Following my early release from Mt. Carmel Medical Center the day before, I had glanced at national news about the "big snowstorm" my doctor had warned was on the way. "They say it'll be a huge one, so we want to get you out of here and home before it hits."

I was all for that. From my sofa, I gazed through the huge picture window that made up most of the front wall of our living room, and watched children scurry into Oakland Elementary School across the street. I wondered if they would soon enjoy a snow day. At dismissal, the kids, puzzled by the unusually warm afternoon, spilled out of the building and tugged off their mittens and hats. Some shucked their coats and stuffed them into backpacks.

"Snowstorm. What snowstorm?" I mumbled as I dozed off.

At 5:30, I heated a bowl of soup. Another rule: only soft foods. Watching the news seemed like a good idea, so I tuned in to a horrific weather forecast. Maps of the entire Midwest swirled with lines called isobars revealing startling low pressures. Suddenly, I took the impending "big snowstorm" seriously, and started to worry about my husband who was attending a graduate class at the University of Akron.

Walter Cronkite was the most trusted newsman in the nation, so when he said, "Blizzard," my mouth went dry. Many people associate blizzards with heavy snowfall, and that can certainly happen. But frightfully high winds and cold temperatures are a blizzard's true calling card.

Unsettled, I opened my front door to take stock. It was like stepping into another world. The unnaturally still air muffled traffic sounds from Clark Street. and the entire atmosphere seemed to hold its breath in anticipation. At 60 degrees, the temperature, at odds with the urgent weather warnings, was much too warm for January. Taking a deep breath, I detected the odor of ozone – odd in the absence of lightning.

Carefully, I walked to the edge of the porch and scanned the skies to the north. Creepy sparkles skittered across the back of my neck and along my shoulders. The whole northern sky glowed a dull, murky green. Rarely can we, at 40 degrees latitude, get a glimpse of the Northern Lights, but there they were.

When my husband came home, he reported a 60 degree temperature and light rain at the university. Later, we watched the 11 o'clock news and the intensified weather warnings. By this time, barometric readings were hovering slightly below 29 millibars of mercury, sliding into dangerous territory.

At midnight, the first blast of wind hit the picture window, vibrating it with the sound of a bass drum. Fearing flying glass, I buried my head under my quilt, but the window held fast. All night and into the morning, the winds howled with furious voices. Finally, at eight o'clock the next morning, our neighborhood lost power. The house chilled rapidly and the world was drowned in white silence – no radio, TV, cycling furnace hum, refrigerator motor, or bubbling teakettle.

Friends, who lived a few blocks away and had a wood burning stove, arrived to take us to a warm room in their home. We opened the front door to a porch knee-deep in snow. I'm still amazed that our friends' Volkswagen made the trip to fetch us to safety. With my husband supporting me on one side and my friend on the other, I trudged to the car. If I hadn't been a week away from major surgery, I'd have called this an adventure.

Although we were able to return home that night, the blizzard howled on until January 27th. When all was said and done, the toll was horrible. Of the 71 people who died as a result of the blizzard, 52 of them were Ohioans. The National Weather Service called the storm a category 5 event – a white hurricane. From January 26 through January 27, the Ohio Turnpike was shut down for the first time ever. To top it off, Ohio State University closed all campuses for the first time in the history of the school.

When I look back at the weather maps that recorded those three days, I marvel that we escaped so lightly. Nature has a way of putting the events of our lives into stark perspective.

A White Christmas...

During WWII, the U.S. Army built a 168-building, 2,000-bed hospital for care of the war's wounded three miles north of Cambridge. This photo was taken at war's end, circa Christmas, 1945. Three months later, having served more than 17,000 wounded veterans, it closed. This facility became the Cambridge State Hospital in May, 1946.

White Stuff

BY BOB LEY

No go in this snow!

We were living in Parkersburg, West Virginia, when the second largest snowfall in the area's recorded history swept over the Ohio Valley in 1950. I was nine. Looking out, we discovered the front door opened in, but the storm door opened out. Drifting snow had reached the top of the doors. It looked strange and would have been funny, until we realized there was no way out.

Rushing to the back door, we found a similar situation.

Dad was in a panic about getting to work… he *never* missed work! Mom tried to tell him it would be okay; no customers would be out today anyway, which did not mollify him one bit.

Of course, school had been called off. My only thoughts were about getting outside to play in the white stuff! Around noon, a group of teen boys offered to shovel us out for a small fee. With one young man standing in snow chest high, shouting back and forth with Dad through closed windows, a deal was made and he *would* get to work!

An hour later, the sidewalk and the door were cleared, the shoveled snow stacked over my head along the sidewalk. Dad, still dressed in his suit and tie, had not given up on getting to work. (I wonder where I get it?) Mom was happy to see him go. His general grumpiness was wearing thin with her. He walked out, only to see snow as high as the car roof and the street impassable. He marched back to the house, finally defeated.

Neighborhood boys came to the door, wanting me to join them. I asked Mom. "Sure, but you have to take your brother," she declared. John was seven and sure to be in our way. Reluctantly (Mom had just pulled another fast one!), I took him along.

We had a grand time building snowmen on porches. Snow forts and tunnels popped up everywhere, which prompted the inevitable snowball fights. Brother John took an icy snowball in the face, which ended the day out for me, too.

At the time, it seemed the snow lasted for months. In reality it was probably two weeks...

but what fun!

A Slow Business Day...

Stoutt's Sandwich & Ice Cream Shop at Dewey Avenue and the Route 40 turn up Tunnel Hill may have had a slow day with this much snow.

Photo courtesy of the Guernsey County History Museum.

In the Snowbanks

BY JOY L. WILBERT ERSKINE

It gives me the shivers even now.

It was a glorious snowfall, that Presidents' Day snowstorm of 2003. Delicate white flakes soared crazily by the windows, riding a spinning, whistling wind, rather than descending sedately in discreet stillness, like any sensible snowflake.

I remember looking out the front window of my home on North 10th Street, marveling at the strength of the storm, then moving to a window on the lee side of the house to spy on fluffy birds huddling amid the snowy branches of the pear tree. They seemed very much like stranded passengers on a holiday gone horribly wrong, shivering and twittering among themselves, waiting worriedly for the next possible flight south.

It was very cold, but the deliciously shivery kind of cold. The kind like when, as a kid, I waited for my turn to barrel headfirst down the slope behind our house. All of us, brothers and sisters, were more excited than frozen, until Mom called us in. Back in the warm kitchen, stripping down, drying off, we realized how icy we really were. Thank goodness for warm blankets and hot chocolate, then we'd beg to go back outside to do it again.

In 2003, too old to go sledding even if there'd been a hill on 10th Street to slide down, I watched the snowflakes fly from the warmth of my armchair, sipping hot chocolate, remembering. After three days, curiosity got the better of me. Venturing out armed with a yardstick, I measured the depth of the snow in our back yard – 19 inches! It was the most snow I'd ever seen from one storm. Freezing cold, I snapped a couple pictures of the yardstick peeking from the snow, then beat a hasty retreat to the mud room, stomping the snow off my boots, and shaking it out of my hood and hair. Not realizing how quickly it would melt, I stepped into a puddle in my socks and did a spontaneous snow dance on the cold linoleum – another deliciously shivery memory to add to my collection.

Cambridge remained shut down for days while I enjoyed a mini-vacation in a quiet little retreat called home. No traffic, no mail, no visitors, just blissful quiet, peace, and solitude. I wished it would never end. It would be several weeks before the last of the snow finally melted away into spring. The Presidents' Day snowstorm of 2003, however, is frozen for all eternity in the snowbanks of my memory.

One-Room School Days...

Richland Township's picturesque Grandview School and snowy hills.
Photo courtesy of the Guernsey County History Museum.

Big Snows I Have Known

BY JUDY SIMCOX

Remembrance of hardships and fun.

The first "big snow" I remember was in New Jersey when I was ten or eleven. It was unusual for us to get more than just a couple of inches at a time, but that snow must have been the best part of two feet, with drifts. The thing I remember most vividly about it was jumping out of the bedroom window into a drift beside the driveway.

Our house was a tract house in a neighborhood of very similar houses. On our block, there were ten houses, and in those ten houses, (actually in only six of them, because childless older couples lived in four), there were 20 children, all but one of them younger than me. Their idea in the aftermath of the snow was to jump off these overhanging roofs between the first and second floors into the best drifts they could aim at. When I discovered how close my backside came to the corner of the central AC unit, I decided against a second jump. I decided against it for my sisters, too. I think my brothers were jumping out of windows at friends' houses, Ritchie's or Petey's.

I remember the big snow here in '78. One of the things I recall most vividly, besides the invasion of the National Guard, God bless 'em, was the "alpine climate" effect observed when driving from town to my parents' hilltop home in Adams Township. Snow was everywhere, of course, but as I traveled up Route 209, the drifts got deeper. It needed plowing every morning after a busy night of drifting back over the road, and again in the afternoon, as the wind didn't stop at dawn. I was staying at my parents' house, since my little house was only accessible with a Herculean effort, or more like a Quinn the Eskimo effort, and would have been easier with reindeer, but not for me.

I would climb up 209, slow but steady, fortunately not meeting too many junctions because I couldn't see over the snowbanks if anyone was coming at me. When I came to Township Road 1624, I turned left, ground up the gravel slope to the driveway and sort of heaved my car into this little niche, where it was off the road, but that's about it. I felt like a good, sensible Ohio driver every time I managed this.

I remember a snowfall once when my daughter was about three and we lived in Martins Ferry. It was respectable, maybe five or six inches, heavy and wet, and it fell during Easter week. My father-in-law, who was a right jolly old elf, hurried out into it and built a snowman nearly six feet tall, with an odd straw hat and a big smile. I have pictures he took of me and the kid beside it, somewhere.

I like snow, especially if I don't have to drive in it. When you walk in it, well wrapped in snuggly outerwear and good boots with traction, you can hear that you can't hear anything. You can catch flakes on your sleeve and actually see how different they all are, if you have the right glasses. Snow falling past streetlights is otherworldly. Snow that piles up deep enough to cover everything – streets, scraggly flower beds, litter, etc. – silent and sparkling, and inviting you to take your dumpy footprints elsewhere, is magical.

Town Under a Coal-Fire Haze...

Snow blankets Cambridge in this view, circa 1920, looking straight up Steubenville Avenue from the vicinity of Coshocton Avenue on the west side of town. The iron bridge shown was replaced long ago. The Guernsey County Courthouse is hazily visible in the background. The haze over the town is likely due to hundreds of coal fires burning to keep homes and buildings warm.

Photo courtesy of the Guernsey County History Museum.

Melting Snow

BY BEVERLY WENCEK KERR

*Snowflakes all around,
and not a drop to drink.*

The big snow shut everything down. That's when Mom and Dad gave thanks they had a coal furnace and bottled gas cooking stove. Sure, we had no lights, but we stayed warm and could cook meals the same as before. Any food that needed refrigerated went outside in containers with snow packed all around them.

The biggest problem was water, as we had switched from the hand pump in the back yard to an electric pump that brought water into the house. Now no water ran from the faucets.

The snowstorm caused many extra tasks, but then Mom and Dad were accustomed to working hard. People in those days had to be self-reliant and able to come up with solutions to their unexpected problems.

Remember, this big, big snow measured over two feet thick all over the countryside. So Mom would go outside and fill up a bucket with snow, bring it in to the bottled gas stove and begin heating it. Often she would set a bucket of snow on a register to start it melting there.

A bucket of snow didn't give very much water, so the process continued all day long. The basic rule said that every ten inches of snow gave one inch of water. That's a lot of melting!

You see, not only did we need water for washing, cooking, and dishes, but we had thousands of thirsty chickens.

My picture of Mom remains clear. She bundled up in her heavy winter coat with a wool scarf on her head, and hands covered with warm work gloves. Black boots went over her shoes and buckled around her ankles.

She would head to the chicken house with a bucket in each hand, as the chickens needed water just the same as we did. Without water, chickens don't grow as fast or lay eggs as well. Chickens are fairly tough critters, so all survived with some tender loving care.

During this very difficult year, electricity remained off for over a week. Mom and Dad had some pretty sore arms by that time from carrying water. As a very young only child, my parents were a bit overprotective of me and didn't want me to help with this process. Still, once in a while, it was fun to go outside and get a bucket of snow to put on the register.

We felt lucky! Lucky to live in a warm house with a stove on which to cook our meals. When it comes right down to it, the little things in life are what's important.

Jingle All the Way...

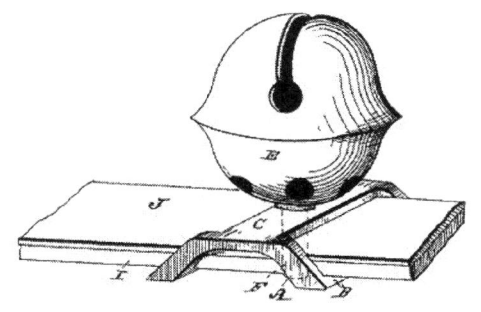

Howard Simons of the Simons Foundry in Cambridge patented this sleigh bell fastener in 1887. It was manufactured at his foundry on the south side of Turner Avenue between Seventh and Eighth Streets.

My First Blizzard

BY MARTHA F. JAMAIL

Snow can be surprisingly warm.

The only thing better than watching a lovely first snowfall, is seeing it through the eyes of your children and grandchildren. I was fortunate enough to be able to do both…with my own children and later with my grandchildren. I have the perfect image of each of them silhouetted against the glass of a window, staring in wonder at snowflakes falling softly from the sky.

I actually didn't see my first snowfall until I was 23 years old. Growing up in the Mississippi Delta, our winters were cold and icy, but snowfall was a rarity. While in elementary school, I often wondered why the winter bulletin boards always depicted children sliding down a snow-covered hill. Not only did we have no snow during the winter, we also had no hills. The Delta was flat land as far as the eye could see.

That first Mississippi snowfall I saw was barely enough to cover the dry leaves on the ground, but I was still able to form 3 little snowballs to build a rudimentary snowman. My cousins and I took lots of pictures to remember that special day.

After I married, my husband and I settled in Cambridge, Ohio, where snowy winters became a fact of life. The most memorable one, though, was the winter of '77-'78. The snow that winter blasted the state, shutting down roads, businesses and closing schools. Many homes lost power, and I remember we used our wood-burner for supplemental heat.

As a teacher I remember marking 18 consecutive days of no school. Fierce winds had blown the snow into five-foot drifts in front of our house. When the winds finally subsided, I decided to venture out with my three-year-old son to see the snow. We bundled up in our snowsuits and when we got to the front yard, we were both amazed at how beautiful and pristine the snow looked. The snowdrift next to the house was practically my height, and I began to scoop out snow with my gloved hands. The consistency of the snow was perfect for forming a snow cave, and soon the opening was large enough for both my son and me to crawl inside. It was surprising how warm it felt as we sat in our cave sheltered from the frigid air. I remember telling my son that the Eskimos were able to stay warm like that in their snow igloos. We even enjoyed a cup of hot chocolate in our snow cave.

After sharing that experience together, I realized that blizzards can certainly disrupt our lives, but their results are often scenes of awesome beauty, and great memories.

Saving It for Summer...

Before the days of electric freezers, one of the best ways to have ice available in the summer was to harvest it for storage during the winter. Here three men harvest ice on the Tuscarawas River, circa 1900.

Mom, I Tore My Pants Again

BY SAMUEL D. BESKET

A stitch in time saves the behind.

A surge of adrenaline shot through my body as I sped down Christopher's Hill. Halfway down the hill, I realized my sled wasn't responding to the controls. No matter how hard I pressed on the rudder bar, it wouldn't turn. A large elm tree was looming larger and larger as I raced toward it. Finally, in desperation, I dragged my left foot, turning the sled and missing the tree by inches. My joy was short-lived as my sled struck a hidden rut. The sled stopped abruptly, but I didn't. One of the many nails sticking up on my seat tore into my overalls as I slid across it, ripping a four-inch gash in the back. After standing up, I felt the tear and realized my pants weren't the only casualty of the ride.

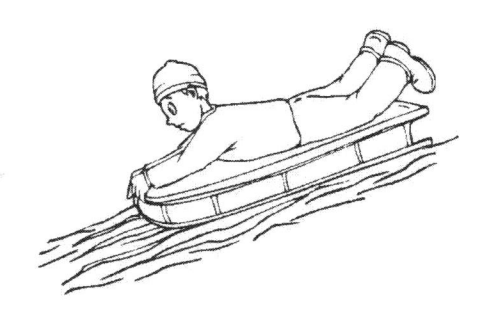

I don't know how many times my mother patched my pants; almost as many times as I patched my sled. My shiny Flexible Flyer wasn't shiny any more. Barely three months ago, it was standing in the window of Burson's Hardware Store; now it looked the worse for wear. The bright red frame was chipped and bent. The seat boards were split and what nails remained were bent or sticking up, but it was the fastest sled on the hill.

Christopher's Hill was the ideal spot for sled riding in our neck of the woods. The top half was extremely steep, then it tapered off into a gradual slope. The only hazards were Mr. Christopher's bull and some frozen cow patties. Years later, we found out he kept the bull in the barn when he saw us sledding.

Not everyone had a sled, so we would ride double. The increased weight increased our speed, which resulted in numerous crashes. The worst crash occurred when we slid into a fresh cow patty. Since my house was across the road from the hill, it was easy for me, not so easy for Mom, to go home, change clothes, and drink some hot chocolate while we thawed out.

Today, no one sled-rides on the hill. Occasionally, after a snow, I will drive by hoping to see a young boy on a Flexible Flyer, but the hill is empty. Mr. Christopher and the kids who sledded there are long gone, but the memories are etched in my mind.

The remains of my sled are in the attic of my storage building. The frame has been straightened and painted. The boards on the wooden frame are still cracked and split, with bent and protruding nails. I intend to leave it that way.

RDWP

A Tough Travel Day...

Light snow was much less a problem for the train in this 1974 picture than was the fact it had just derailed beside the old train station at Cambridge.

Photo courtesy of the Guernsey County History Museum, Adair Collection

Stranded

BY HARRIETTE MCBRIDE ORR

It's good to always be prepared.

Dear Readers,

There were several big snows in Cambridge in 1977 and '78. I worked third shift at Champion Spark Plug, which meant we were on the road in the dark after most people had gone to bed. Our drive home early in the morning was often before the snowplows cleared the roads.

One night we were going to work, even though roads had been closed except for emergency traffic. Barb Conrath lived on 18th Street and she volunteered to pick us all up on Clark Street. Brenda Pennington walked from Edgeworth, and Shirley Patterson and I from North 11th Street. It wasn't too long before we got stopped by the law. He wanted to know just where we were headed, and after we told him, we got a lecture about being careful and he waved us on.

Barb drove a heavy old Chrysler that got around in the snow pretty well, but that winter it would often just stop running, without warning. Twice, we broke down right in front of a bar. We got ribbed about stopping at bars on our way home. One day Barb's car caught fire, and that ended our bar stops.

We had lots of white knuckles when it came to sliding up and down Tunnel Hill out of Cambridge, but we always made it. No one got hurt, so we can look back and laugh about those adventures.

There went the alarm. Looking over at the clock I

saw that it was 12:30 pm – way too early for me to get up. My usual wake-up time was 3 pm. Then I remembered, we had to take son, Kim, back to school at Alliance, Ohio's, Mount Union College. Just as my feet hit the floor, the front door opened and Duchess the dog started barking. The kids were home.

"Mom, Mom, are you up yet? It quit snowing and we need to take Kim back to school. Did you forget?" yelled Tina.

"No, no, I am getting up. Just called the State Patrol to see if the roads are clear, and they said the roads were open all the way. Let's get the car packed."

There had been a record-breaking blizzard over the weekend, and it had dumped several inches of snow over Ohio, paralyzing much of the state. The National Guard was out helping clear the roads.

I had worked at Champion Spark Plug all night. Only people who lived nearby had been able to make it out Route 40 to the plant for work. We had worked with a skeleton shift.

Son, Kim, was a member of the wrestling team at Mount Union and they were having wrestle-offs that afternoon at 4 pm. He had to make the event in order to qualify for the next meet.

The roads were not clear, but passable. In Canton we turned off I-77, heading northeast toward Alliance. It was just 2 pm, and we ended up in a stream of traffic behind a snowplow.

"We've got it made," I told the kids. "This is going to be the way to go. That snowplow will get us through."

As we drove along, one of the girls pointed out that there was no traffic in the other two lanes heading west. They were full of snow. "Oh, don't worry," I said, "We're okay, we've got a snowplow up front."

All at once our lane of traffic started to slow and we came to a complete stop. We had just passed an exit. The snowplow driver came back to explain to us that he was going to make a turn around so that we could get back to the exit. The snow up ahead was too deep for the plow to get through.

Slowly the plow got a turn-around plowed out for us, but as we were preparing to get on the exit, a large loaded steel truck headed up the exit in front of us, and became stuck, or broke down. No one could get up or down the exit.

There we were, out in the country seven miles from Mount Union. It was snowing again and the wind was bitter cold. The snowplow crew came back and told each car that they had called the airport to send help. They didn't know how long it would take for help to arrive and pull the truck out.

There were several people gathering outside our car. One of the guys came over and asked if anyone was going to school. He said they were headed to Mount Union and had decided to walk the seven miles.

Kim said he wanted to walk with them and started handing out his clothes for people who needed more warmth. Socks became mittens for those who had no gloves. This was long before cell phones and I was worried about them walking so far, and not knowing if they made it or not. There were around ten of them, so I felt there would be safety in numbers. Tina and Candy hugged Kim goodbye and off he went, and we began our wait.

I was glad I had filled the car up with gas before we left Cambridge, because we had to run the car to keep warm. Finally, around six in the evening, a huge wrecker truck arrived from the airport along with a gigantic snowplow. They went right to work clearing the roadway and getting the truck towed out of there.

It was 7:30 pm by the time we got up the exit and into a town nearby. The girls and I were cold and starved, not to mention that we needed a bathroom. NOTHING WAS OPEN! As we got closer to Canton we found a small diner. Getting something to eat and using the bathroom made the ride home much more comfortable.

I had to go in to work at Champion at eleven pm. I must say that was a long night, but I had plenty to talk about.

We found that Kim, who we had worried about being out in the cold, was at school around an hour after he left us. After all that had happened, Kim had been too late for wrestle-offs so he didn't get placed. The coach was upset he had not called to let him know he would be late. Remember...no cell phones. We had been so worried about Kim walking to school, yet there he was, safe and sound and inside where it was warm, hours before we were, even though he didn't make wrestle-offs.

We all learned a valuable lesson from this experience. It pays to be prepared.

Another Way to Get Stranded...

In 1913, Cambridge became virtually an island during the worst flood event in Ohio history. This photo of the First Street area in Cambridge shows distant Brown's Heights on the other side of flood waters.

The "Boys"

BY BOB LEY

A tale of two immigrants.

Pete and Jim Nicholakis were neighbors on North Eighth Street. They were cousins, retired, and lifelong friends. They played cards most evenings. The games were intense and taken seriously by both of them.

Each morning, the two would meet on the sidewalk and trek the eight blocks to downtown Cambridge. Even if the game from the night before had been contentious, or caused almost any real or imagined offense, the walk still went on, but with each cousin on opposite sides of the street, not speaking to each other. If the results of the game had been amicable, Jim and Pete walked together, talking animatedly, hands and arms waving.

Their first stop was generally a visit to the lunch counter at Newberry's, each one ordering coffee but seldom drinking it, and never bringing up last night's game. A truce of sorts. Often, my store was another stop on their morning-in-town outing, just for small talk and bantering with me and my associate, Paul Coss. Occasionally, the conversation would turn to helping us wait on a customer by telling him how nice he'd look in whatever item he was considering. Their technique was so transparent it usually had us all laughing.

Tales of the old days, another of their favorite topics, brought forth many funny stories, most often at the expense of the one not telling it. Strange, but this kind of teasing was okay with them. The trip to town must have been therapeutic. Going back up Eighth Street hill for their lunch at home resolved any final hard feelings. Bidding the other "good day," each went home for lunch to await the evening card game.

Every Christmas, Pete's wife, Sophie, brought me a tray of homemade Greek pastries, including my favorite, baklava. The note attached was always a variation of "Thank you for putting up with the 'boys.'"

Jim and Pete, first generation Greek-Americans, worked hard, started businesses, and taught their children the great values cherished by them both. Most of all, they lived life with a great sense of humor. God speed, 'boys!'

Greek to Me...

A 1910 Guernsey County promotional booklet included this picture of Pleasant City's Greek Orthodox Church. It's still there, known as St. Michael's Byzantine Catholic Church today.

Photo courtesy of the Guernsey County History Museum.

An Immigrant's Story

Told by Freda Iser

Written by Martha Jamail

It's important to learn the lessons of history.

Freda Iser has had a remarkable life. Born in Petersdorf, Moravia, in 1936, she still remembers an unusual event that happened to her as a seven-year-old. She was standing in the public square when a loud speaker began making an announcement about Hitler. She raised her arm in the "Heil Hitler" salute as her parents had instructed her, when a convoy of Russian army trucks happened to be passing through. One of the trucks stopped, and a Russian soldier got out and approached her. Seeing how frail she looked, he offered her a paper cone filled with sugar cubes. Then he admonished her, "No more Heil, Hitler!" as he made a slicing gesture with his finger across his throat.

The Russian soldiers in that first group passing through Petersdorf had been kind to the people, but the second group was vicious. They wanted to convert everyone to communism. They raped young girls, and took women and their children to work camps, where they were forced to clean and repair the railroad tracks damaged in the war.

Young men and women, including Freda's older sister, were made to dig up coffins in the cemeteries and remove jewelry, rings, gold fillings from teeth, and any other valuables they could find. When their gory tasks were completed, they were offered a cigarette to distract them, while other soldiers shot them in the back, and buried them in the very same holes they had dug. Freda's sister, Edith, was very fortunate, though. Her life was spared because she spoke both Russian and German and was used as a translator.

Soon after the war ended, Freda and her family fled to Munich, Germany, to escape communism. They were forced to travel by train, in cattle wagons packed with over 100 people in each car. The adults stood crammed into each other with no room to move. Only the corners were left open, where everyone piled their coats so the children would not have to lie on the floor.

As refugees, Freda and her family were unwanted by the Germans. Freda's father had been a railroad engineer, but was unable to get a job because he was considered too old to work. He was 50 years old at the time. Their family had very little to eat, and when Freda was 11 years old, she was hospitalized for a month due to malnutrition. Her brother, who was 7 years older than she, had been forced to serve on the front lines for Hitler. Her 16-year-old sister finally got a job in a textile factory, and was able to support the family.

Freda's husband-to-be, Louis Iser, was an American soldier stationed in Germany. Impressed with her beauty and demeanor, he asked her out many times over a period of two years, but she refused him each time. When she finally decided to go out with him, he proposed on their first date, and she surprised him by saying "Yes!" Two weeks later, he came with a marriage license and papers for her parents to sign giving their permission. He was scheduled to return soon to the States, so they went to the chaplain on the base and were married on December 5, 1955. In Germany, you weren't considered legally married unless you were married by the bürgermeister (comparable to our mayor). So on February 15, 1956, they were married again. In addition to that, she was also required to undergo a police report to ensure she didn't have a criminal record.

Freda was apprehensive about her trip to America and wondered what foods she should bring with her. Her friends told her not to worry – in America, everything you'd want to eat came in a can. While they were stationed in Monterey, California, Freda's neighbors were very kind and helpful to her. She wanted to repay them for their thoughtfulness so she decided to bake a cake and have them over for coffee.

In Germany, baking powder came in an envelope, so of course her German recipe called for an envelope of baking powder. Freda tried to remember how much would be in an envelope and guessed 5 teaspoons. So she scooped 5 teaspoons of baking powder into her cake batter. Of course the cake grew and grew as it baked, until it practically filled the oven and then collapsed on itself, making a big mess. She had to do something quickly, so she went to the commissary and saw a large can with a picture of a delicious chocolate cake on it. She bought it and also got a package of sandwich cookies, just in case someone didn't want chocolate cake. When she arrived home, she opened the can, but instead of chocolate cake, it was a can of Crisco shortening! She and her guests had a good laugh over it while they enjoyed coffee and sandwich cookies. America was full of surprises…and good neighbors, too.

Freda and her husband, Louis, enjoyed 47 wonderful years together. He was able to enjoy the birth of their five children, five of their seven grandchildren, and one of their ten great-grandchildren, before he passed away.

In closing, Freda shared that as soon as she gained her citizenship, she registered to vote, and has voted in every election as a proud American.

In a Surrey with the Fringe on Top…

Some proud Americans rode down Wheeling Avenue in this surrey in the early 1890s, perhaps in a Fourth of July parade. The building at right, 731 Wheeling Avenue, looks much the same today as it did then. No longer the Henry Greenwold Dry Goods Store, it deliciously houses Nothing But Chocolate today.

Photo courtesy of the Guernsey County History Museum.

Chan Gee, Laundryman or Tea Merchant?

BY RICK BOOTH

The penalty of success.

"I am a tea merchant. I import the tea from China," explained Chan Gee to the San Francisco customs agent, stationed dockside.

"Yes, yes, yes. That's not the problem. Are you also a laundryman?" queried the frustrated official.

"No. No laundry. Just tea. I am tea importer. Only tea," Chan implored. To admit to being a laundryman, or even participating in a laundry business in 1901, was perilous for anyone from China seeking entry into the U.S. Stuck for more than two weeks on a ship tied up in San Francisco Harbor, Chan Gee's effort to convince the agent he was really just a tea merchant seemed the only way to get home – home to Coshocton, Ohio.

"Mr. E. J. Miller, our Columbus customs man, sent Inspector Smiley out to this 'Coshocton' place, you see," the agent explained, eyeing Chan for a telltale reaction. "He asked about your business there. What do you think people said?"

"Tea. They say I import the tea. I sell the tea," blurted Chan excitedly.

Frowning, the agent continued, "Uh-huh. And they also said you own a laundry business." He paused to let the words sink in. "You were gone too long.

A laundryman can't leave the country for more than a year and then come back in. That's the law now. You were gone for… well it says here… twenty-eight months. That's too long. If you were only a tea merchant, you could come in. But not if you do laundry, too. The law is very clear about that."

"Laundry was long time ago. Long time. Now I am tea merchant," Chan countered, feeling his chance at re-entering America slipping away. He had tucked away money for a dozen years to go back to the land of his birth, but never expected such trouble as this re-entering his adopted country.

"No, they say you still own the business. It's on North Fifth Street. They were starching shirts when Mr. Smiley walked in. I have to follow the law. I'm afraid you'll have to go back to China. When this ship sails again, out through that Golden Gate, you'll be on it."

"But did my friends write to you?" Chan asked wistfully, sadly.

"Oh, yes. You do have friends, and good ones. The postmaster, the banker, and the newspaper editor… yes, they all wrote. They all say you're a very good man, too – a laundry man! They want you back, but there's nothing I can do."

"Did Mr. Mackey write?"

"Yes. And I understand Attorney Mackey and his wife were also fond of you. They taught you to read and write English it said in the note. Is that right?"

"Yes, yes. I only know little English when I start laundry business in Cambridge. Fifteen years ago I go there. I work hard – long, long hours – in basement on Main Street. The Mackeys, they very good to me. Good man. Good woman. Mrs. Mackey taught me, too."

"Then why did you leave that town?" inquired the agent, checking his pocket watch impatiently.

"Business, sir. It was business! Make second laundry in Coshocton. Let cousin run Cambridge business."

"Well, Mr. Gee, this ship won't sail for at least another week, I'd guess. If I hear anything new from Washington before then, I'll let you know. But if I don't, may you have a pleasant voyage home."

The foregoing conversation, or at least one much like it, really did apparently occur in the spring of 1901. In scattered columns of newspaper reports, it is clear that Cambridge, Ohio, once had a much-liked and very successful Chinese laundryman named Chan Gee. He arrived in the city around 1886, working in the basement of the building at the northwest corner of Seventh Street and Wheeling Avenue in Cambridge. A Cambridge attorney named J. H. Mackey, along with his wife, taught Chan Gee to read and write in English. He was successful enough to start a second laundry business in Coshocton. It also seems he really did have a side business importing tea.

Chan Gee was a victim of his own success. He made enough money to take a trip back to China to see relatives in December, 1898. But in his two-year absence, laws and regulations concerning Chinese immigration changed. By the time he returned in the spring of 1901, he was part of a federally-excluded group – the Chinese laundrymen.

Newspaper accounts of 1901 tell of Mr. Chan Gee being held essentially a prisoner on a ship in San Francisco Bay while federal agents checked out his story of being a tea merchant, not a laundryman.

The ultimate fate of Chan Gee is not clear from old newspaper records. No article yet found says whether China or Coshocton was to be his next home. But an article in a Coshocton newspaper in 1902 gives a clue. Curious about the Chinese men operating the laundry on Fifth Street, the newspaper interviewed and reported on them. The two men operating the Coshocton laundry a year and a half after Chan Gee tried to argue his way back into the United States were named Quong Sing and Tom Gee. No mention is made of Chan Gee, the business founder, in the paper.

It is likely that Chan Gee never did succeed at returning to Ohio from his long homeland visit. He left behind, though, many who thought well of him, including the couple in Cambridge who taught him to read and write the English language, and quite a few prominent citizens of Coshocton. He was once an immigrant success story, and then a victim of that very success. Chan Gee left behind much more than starched shirts and clean trousers. He left behind good friends and fond memories. Though perhaps he never returned, at least in two towns of Southeastern Ohio, he indelibly left his mark.

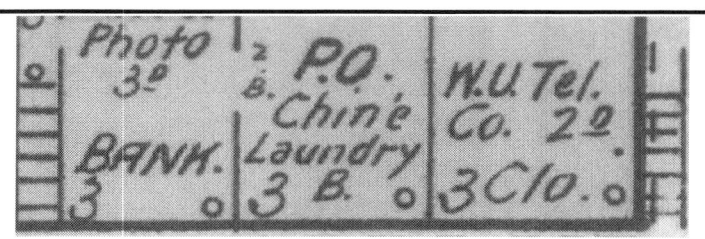

RDW

Chan Gee ran his laundry beneath the post office at 651 Wheeling Avenue as of 1892. The telegraph office and a bank were next door.

Babushka Power

BY BEVERLY WENCEK KERR

Give it a whirl!

My grandmother, who we called Baba, often wore a babushka. This square cotton scarf covered her hair and tied under her chin. As youngsters, most of the girls in our family also wore babushkas. Sometimes I still wear one.

But you have to wonder where this tradition began. Turns out the word "babushka" has several meanings. In Eastern Europe, it means grandmother. Is that how we got the term Baba to refer to our grandmother, who was from Czechoslovakia?

Babushka also denotes that scarf that covers the head. The women of Eastern Europe all wore this scarf, and when they came to this country, the scarf came with them. While some were a solid color, most scarves contained floral or other interesting patterns, often depicting folklore in bright colors. Fancier scarves might include intricate embroidery patterns.

Back in 1975, the Pittsburgh Pirates realized that many of their fans came from Eastern Europe so they asked all the women in the area to come to a baseball game wearing their babushkas. As a good luck charm, the women would take off their babushkas and twirl them in the air. The Pirates called this Babushka Power.

On one Babushka Night, the Pirates gave away black and gold babushkas to every woman that attended the game. Since it was Ladies Night, they also got a $1.35

discount on their tickets. This was at a time when box seats were $4.50! That promotion brought 12,345 women to the game, and with their Babushka Power, the Pirates beat the Phillies 8-1 in front of 43,260 fans.

The Babushka Brigade was formed! For a mere $1.49, ladies could purchase a ticket to another Ladies Night game and receive a black and gold babushka provided by Murphy's Mart with the Pirates' logo and "Babushka Brigade" stamped on it. What a bargain!

A Pittsburgh area Ford distributor, East Hills Ford Sales, used "Babushka Power" in their advertisements and gave free babushkas to customers. Large numbers of women flocked to the game wearing their babushkas. They even crowned one lucky lady as Babushka Queen. There's no doubt that the Babushka Power led to the Pittsburgh Steelers' Terrible Towel, which was also waved at games for good luck.

Perhaps a little Babushka Power would help me write more stories. Excuse me, while I get my babushka.

In Quest of Coal...

Names from Eastern Europe were common in Guernsey County mines. This picture shows part of a local mine's employee time log in 1935. The men who actually dug the coal aren't listed in the log because they were paid by the ton, not by the hours they worked. The four employees listed here are remarked as performing "Timber" work, putting in the wooden supports that helped prevent ceiling collapse.

The Fourth of July in Kipling, Ohio

BY HARRIETTE MCBRIDE ORR

Proud to be an American.

At the turn of the 20th century, my grandfather R.P. Lanning, known as RP, owned, in conjunction with Mary and Jack Burris, the general stores at Kings Mine and Kipling, Ohio. The family lived right up the street from the store in Kipling. I was told many times how Grandpa loved the 4th of July and the celebration on that day. It was a time when the whole community came together.

Since this was a mining town, there were several nationalities that would gather on the 4th of July. They came to this country in hopes of making a better living than they had been able to do in the "Old Country" across the Atlantic. Polish, Hungarian, Italian, Lithuanian, Bohemian, Irish, and many Czech and English, made up the Kipling community which was the first to grow up surrounding a coal field. The miners were poorly paid, most not making more than twenty dollars for a two week period, but it was much more than they could have made in the "Old Country."

The mine at Kipling, located along the Baltimore and Ohio Rail Road, was known as the Klondyke, and employed 150 workers at the time. It was owned by the Loomis-Moss Coal

Company. Mine workers from Cambridge walked the four miles or rode the work trains for ten cents. For the Fourth of July celebration, the early work train that day delivered the dry ice from Cambridge for making ice cream. Kids came to the store with their wagons and loaded up with dry ice and salt to take home so the cranking of the ice cream could start. The fireworks RP ordered had come in on the train the day before. That was his favorite part of the celebration and he went all out to make sure he bought the best fireworks they had to offer.

The Methodist Church ladies would get the church ready for the onslaught of people and food. The older boys were set to work outside in the church yard, creating makeshift tables from sawhorses and wood planks. The women covered these tables with sheets and bouquets of fragrant wildflowers. Chairs were brought out and all was made ready.

Families started arriving in the afternoon, with baskets of food and blankets to be spread out in the churchyard so they could sit on the ground. The men at the mine worked until late afternoon. As soon as they got the coal dust washed off, most headed for the beer down on the loading dock. Most of the ladies spent their time at the church tending the food and small children.

The kids ran off to play games such as sack races, tag, hoops, marbles, and hide-and-seek.

When it was time to eat, the church bell rang, calling everyone together. As Justice of the Peace, RP welcomed everyone and gave the blessing. Food had been set out on the tables and people filled their plates with fried chicken, noodles, potato salad, sauerkraut and kielbasas, cabbage rolls, pickled eggs and beets, lemonade, tea, and coffee.

When it came time for desserts, there were berry cobblers, nut rolls, and all kinds of cakes and cookies to be topped off with ice cream. The freezers were brought out and everyone was invited to dig in.

As dinner was ending, some of the guys who played musical instruments got together in front of the church and started playing familiar songs, and soon everyone was singing along. "My Bonnie Lies Over The Ocean," "Danny Boy," and "Daisy, Daisy," were some of the favorites.

As the evening wore on, the band left the churchyard and headed down the street, setting up in front of the store building. There they struck up the lively Slovak, polka and schottische tunes. Soon people young and old were dancing in the street. RP got out his fiddle and called some square dances with polka music in between sets.

As it started to get dark, RP turned the music and square dance calling over to the polka band, and he and some of the men went across the railroad tracks to finish setting up the fireworks. They set off a few rockets, and when they had the crowd's attention, the band struck up the National Anthem. Everyone stood, men and boys with hats off, and all with hands over their hearts. If they knew the words, they joined in the singing. Many did not speak English, but they stood with respect. As the song ended, a great cheer went up from the crowd and the boom, bang of the fireworks took over – a perfect ending to a perfect day .

Harvest in 1955

BY BETSY TAYLOR

Pitching in on the farm.

My grandparents married and lived for a short time in the Village of New Concord. Since Grandpa was a farmer from Pennsylvania, he scouted the area for suitable acreage and found land west of Cambridge.

The land, part of a much larger farm in the 1800s, had an interesting history. During the 1800s it was common for parents to banish a daughter who became pregnant out of wedlock. Some young women and their children were simply abandoned in disgrace. Some were sent away to relatives who might take them in. Others were exiled but supported by money from home. Still others were managed in more creative ways.

It was unusual for a disgraced daughter and her child to remain in the community, but the previous owners of Grandpa's property had set aside a corner of their farm and built a small house for the young woman. The symbolic placement of the house was as far away from the family residence as possible, effectively stressing her shame, while also emphasizing her family's Christian charity. Despite its history, my grandparents with their three little girls, moved into the house.

As my grandparents' family grew, the tiny house underwent additions. Two rooms became four, a step-down kitchen was built around a pump that brought cool water from the well, and a second story was eventually constructed. My mom, my sisters, and I visited every Sunday and enjoyed the changes. I was in high school when a bathroom finally became part of the structure. Before that, we traveled across the yard to an outhouse for necessary visits.

    I was six years old in the summer of 1955, and probably remember that year's harvest best because I was allowed to sit on top of a mountain of unshelled corn in the bed of Grandpa's pickup. I scrambled to the top of the pile and reigned over my subjects while my mom shouted, "That's enough! Come down now. And be careful!"

    Harvest for area farmers meant renting equipment, and as a group, sharing the cost and the labor. My grandparents raised acres of corn that had to be harvested in a short period of time. Everyone, including my mom, was called to help. We lived in Cambridge, so at daybreak, we set off to pitch in.

    From the porch I watched the huge reaper scrape its way, row by row, through nearby cornfields, and saw the shower of ears fall into a waiting bin. Inside the house, the tiny kitchen was bustling as the women, my aunts, grandma, and mom, readied food for the hungry workers. Biscuits hot from the oven, chickens that had been pecking in the barnyard that morning, mashed potatoes and gravy, hot green beans, and bowls of corn were all topped off with freshly baked cherry pie. Hot food in September? Of course. My grandma considered cold sandwiches insufficiently hearty for the tasks at hand.

    My job was to follow orders and stay out of the way. During the late afternoon, I was set to the task of husking. That evening, my itchy, scratchy hands were treated to a thorough dose of witch hazel. I think that's still an ingredient in Corn Huskers' Lotion.

Years later, when I reminded Grandpa of those days of hard physical labor, he reminded me of the great meals. "I wouldn't have had it any other way," he said contentedly.

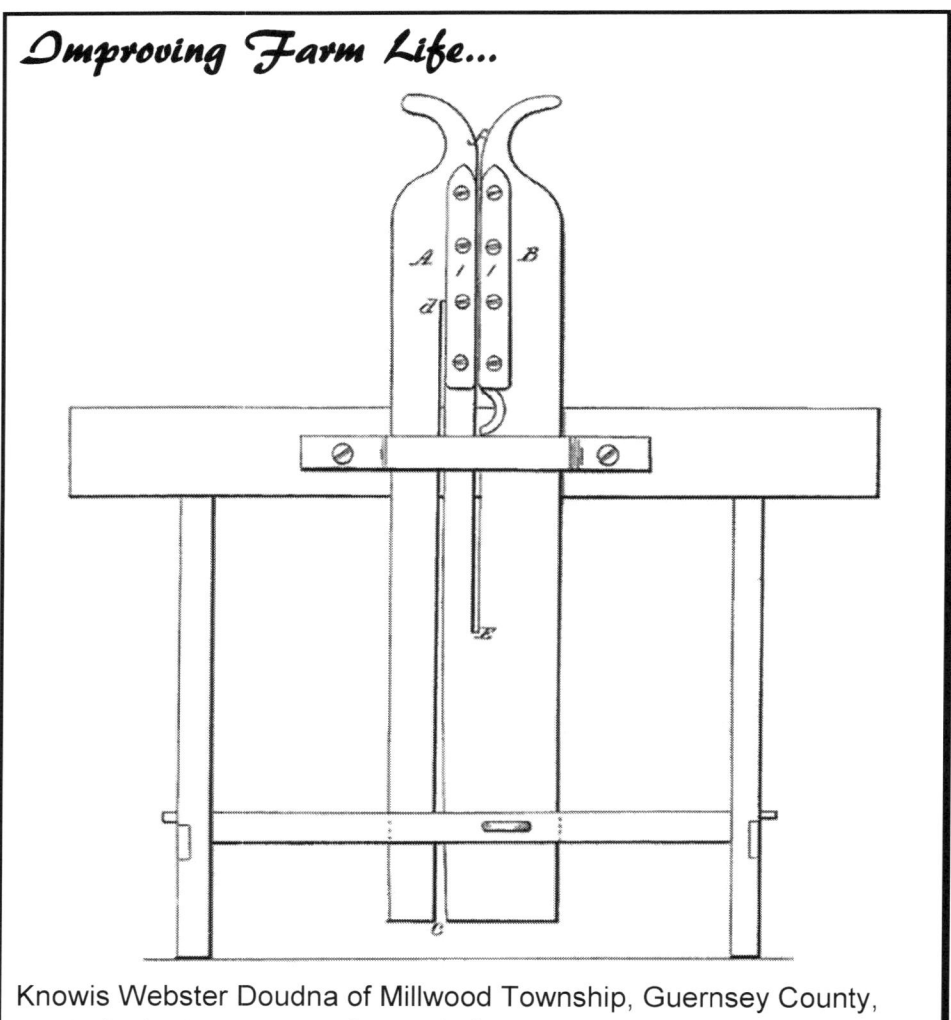

Improving Farm Life...

Knowis Webster Doudna of Millwood Township, Guernsey County, wanted a better way to strip seeds from broom-corn and sorghum at harvest. He patented this seed-stripper in 1866.

I Never Lived on a Farm

BY JUDY SIMCOX

But living in the country comes close.

I never lived on a farm. In New Jersey, I lived in a house built on former farmland, in a tract of houses, row on row, that were all very much alike. The house my parents built when we came to Guernsey County was on former farmland, too. There were none like it nearby, or much closer than the Long Island Sound, which was my mother's intent.

Just over the hill and across the creek was the house of the farmer who sold the land. In between were two barns, one his, worn and weathered, full of years of animal-y goings on, and one ours, very new but already piled high with hay bales, and populated by 4H projects.

One summer day I helped bale and heave bales of hay onto a homemade flatbed. The farmer and his boys, and a couple of my brothers worked several days on this task, but I, only one. I learned that I could heave bales onto the flatbed at the first level, but no higher. I also learned how prickly and scratchy hay was, and stubble, too, and how these conditions were aggravated by sweat. But what caused me to retire from the field was when I saw a nest of baby birds and their frantic parents face the huge tires of the tractor. I screeched, thinking the work would stop and a rescue would be affected. I tried to think what I could do about it, and when the guys noticed what was happening and pretty much shrugged it off, I started to cry and ran off. Such things are common and can't be helped, I guess, like a storm blowing a nest out of a tree, but I just didn't like to bear witness.

I did a few other farm things in the couple of years I lived in the country. Our family created a vegetable garden, and I discovered firsthand just what kind of hindrance a small child "helping" can be. I shouldn't generalize. Perhaps it was just the one, but this kid didn't want to pick up stones out of the dirt I was raking and chopping. He wanted to rake with me, close in front of me with his hands on the rake handle with mine. He also wanted to chop with me, which involved bringing a spade down on big clods with some force, and was a little more difficult. Hoeing and weeding were just as boring as they ever have been, but we did get vegetables. We got nowhere near enough to last a family the winter, and I leave it to you to guess which species produced most prolifically.

I learned to can things, although I would always be dubious about my own products. I did things carefully and correctly, boiling everything to a fare-thee-well, but fortunately never faced the choice of surviving or not on my products. I made pickles out of many odd things, and jam, mostly in the freezer. I look back on these experiences and say, "Why?"

I learned how the woods contain snakes, and sometimes the garage did, too. I learned that all turtles are not "box" – some are "snap," and aptly named. I learned that ponies are way smarter than horses, maybe smarter than dogs, and maybe smarter than me. My mother had been wise to downplay my fanatical campaign to own a horse when I was 12 and lived in suburban New Jersey.

I learned you could almost see the little town where our school was, from a window high in the back of the house, but unless you could fly, you'd be the best part of an hour getting there. I learned the arcane mysteries of a party line. I wouldn't have made a good farmer. They have to work too hard, and I salute them for it.

A Pioneer's Success...

In 1806, a young Quaker named John Hall bought land just east of today's Quaker City. He was, in fact, the first Quaker to settle in that wilderness area. He and his farm attracted other Quakers to the area. In time, this led to the founding of the nearby city, which was originally known as Millwood. The township there retains that name. The farm John Hall started is shown here, as drawn circa 1882.

A Menace of a Rooster

BY HARRIETTE MCBRIDE ORR

Where is he now? Who knows?

Five-year-old Ellis awoke to noises coming from the kitchen, and Mother calling her name for breakfast. Before going downstairs, she used the family chamber pot, located in the hallway between the bedrooms. It was better than having to scurry to the privy several yards from the house.

As usual, Dad and Grandpa were out in the barn milking, while Mother was getting breakfast ready. Ellis found a pan of warm water with Camay soap, and clean clothes waiting for her behind the pot-bellied stove in the sitting room. She washed and quickly dressed, ready for breakfast.

When the men came in, they washed up at the dry sink, while mother poured tea. Ellis got a half cup of milk, filled up with tea and sugar, and a bowl of corn flakes.

Dad had a ritual every morning, and Ellis never grew tired of watching. Slowly, he dotted his toast with chunks of butter, cut precisely off his fork. Then, he generously covered the toast with sugar, then hot tea. Next, he cut the toast into bite size pieces with a dot of butter on each bite. This was his version of "milk toast." He topped this off with meat and a bowl of hot "Mother's Oats."

After breakfast, Mother called, "Ellis, it's time to gather eggs. Get your basket."

"Do I have to, Mother?" she pleaded.

"Yes, now get your basket. I can use your help."

Ellis had always liked gathering eggs, but not now. The old rooster had decided he liked to flap Ellis. So far, Mother had been able to scare him off every time he tried.

Today, the rooster waited until they passed below his perch on the roof of the second chicken coop. As Mother stepped inside, down he flew, landing on Ellis's shoulders, and pecking her on the head while wildly flapping his wings and digging his sharp claws into her shoulders. Ellis was actually scared speechless. It took a while for Mother to come to her aid, as she was hard of hearing and didn't know what was happening.

Ellis wildly swung the basket over her head, trying to knock the rooster off, and eggs went flying everywhere. She finally got her voice back and was able to yell for help. Mother screamed when she saw what was happening, and Dad came running and knocked the rooster off. Ellis was crying, with eggs and broken shells dripping from her hair and face. The old rooster just went a few feet away, proudly strutting, and scratching the ground, all the while keeping his eye on Ellis. Dad hugged her close and in turn eyed the old rooster.

"Don't you worry, honey, he won't ever hurt you again," he promised.

And the rooster? Did he end up as Sunday dinner? No one ever said, but he was never seen strutting his stuff again.

That nasty encounter in the chicken yard caused Ellis to have a deep fear of chickens, and anything with feathers and claws. Even as a grownup, Ellis never liked chickens, alive or cooked. Now pushing eighty years of age, she still has ill feelings | when it comes to chickens.

News to Crow About...

The Guernsey Jeffersonian newspaper of November 22, 1844, published in Old Washington at that time, celebrated the news that Maine had voted for Democrat James K. Polk for president with this illustration of a triumphant rooster and the following verse:

> Oh, take your time, old Rooster,
> My gallant bird and strong;
> Oh, clap your wings, bold Chapman,
> And crow out loud and long!!

Summer Visits

BY JOY L. WILBERT ERSKINE

Milking cows and raising kids.

I'm a city girl and I love it, but every summer growing up I visited country cousins whose family ran a dairy farm. The fresh air, change of scenery, unfamiliar activities, everything we did on those visits, turned into experiences I'll always remember. The cleanliness of the cows, barn, and milk house never failed to impress me. Uncle Roy let me help scrub the milk cans, then fill them with fresh milk for the milk truck to haul away.

The best part of my summer visits was getting to pet the calves, or "hummies," as Aunt Marie always called them. The cows, with those milking machines attached to their teats and their noses buried in the grain trough, were fascinating too, but they could be ornery. The thought of a big hoof stomping on my foot kept me at a safe distance. The babies were much more lovable and more my size, although a tramp from even little hooves didn't feel so good. Most often, milking time found me on the fence surrounding the barn lot, trying to keep the boys from shoving me off into the muck. Chasing barn cats or climbing into the hay mow were more fun anyway.

Another great thing about being on the farm was the food. My aunt, a terrific cook, had lots of home-grown meat, milk, vegetables, and fruit to work with. We always ate well during our stay. I especially loved her homemade cherry pie with ice cream. The cherries came from two tall trees beside the lane as you drove into the farmstead. The ice cream was hand cranked from the farm's milk, eggs, and fruit. My uncle's family stayed busy all day, every day—milking cows, tending chickens, plowing or spraying fields, repairing tractors or fences, helping the neighbors, or tending to other chores. I got the fun part—riding along and taking it all in.

My father's mother (we called her "Mammy") lived in a little house at the top of the farm lane, where the cherry trees grew. No day was complete without a visit there. Her home consisted of two tiny bedrooms, a small living room, a big kitchen with an ample table, and a basement, where she kept her home-canned foods and did her laundry in a wringer washer. I don't think I ever remember Mammy without an apron on, except on Sundays, when she wore it until the last second before going out the door to church. Sitting around the kitchen table, munching on home baked farm house cookies—thick vanilla puddles of goodness, washed down with fresh milk from the farm—or savoring homemade ice cream with fresh berries, was always a welcome treat!

Out back of the house, a line full of freshly laundered clothes always flapped in the breeze. Nearby, a small outhouse, equipped with the necessary Sears catalog, hosted spiders and flies anxious to catch you with your drawers down. Generally, my escape plan involved waiting to use Aunt Marie's indoor toilet later.

With the farm work done, dinner over, and dishes washed, we kids usually spent the evening playing games on the floor or chasing around outside under the pole light while the adults relaxed over coffee, talking about the events of the day. On Friday, auction nights, there'd be a drive to the Crossroads Auction. There, we visited with people we knew, ate farm-fresh sausage sandwiches and French fries, listened to the auctioneer, and checked out anything new in the farm stands. My favorite stop was the Amish bulk candy vendor. For a few cents a pound, we could get a small bag of goodies to share on the way home.

Such good memories! Thank goodness this city girl was smart enough to enjoy life on the farm too.

'Neath Pennsylvania Skies...

Carrie Mae (Warfel) Wilbert, alias "Mammy," the author's grandmother. And yes, she's wearing her apron.

Strawberry Time

BY BEVERLY WENCEK KERR

Kissed by the sun.

Mom rose early to pick strawberries before the day's heat made it uncomfortable. Often a fox would be having a juicy early morning treat when she arrived. "Scoot," she'd shout. She didn't mind his having a snack as there were five acres of strawberries, but didn't want his company.

Dressed in her favorite housedress, she picked berries for hours each day during June and into July. Mom never picked more than one row at a time and picked it thoroughly of all ripe berries.

She carried a wooden hod with her that held eight quart baskets of berries. A berry hod has a handle that reaches from end to end to make it easier to carry the quarts of berries. With her quick hands, it didn't take long to fill a quart.

You would think that each basket was being prepared for a picture, as she wanted them to look perfect. She collected the largest, prettiest berries in one basket. Then when a basket was about full, she would top it with the prettiest, biggest, reddest berries.

All berries would not be placed in the baskets that were for customers. Only the completely ripe and perfect berries went in a basket that would be sold. The blemished ones were used by the family for jam and pies.

Most June days, except Sundays, Mom worked from dawn to dusk picking berries. With a little help, about 300 quarts of berries were picked each day. Her fingers would be red from strawberry stain.

Berries sold for 75 cents a quart. Different varieties ripened at different times. Ozark Beauty produced a large, brilliant red berry early in the summer, while Tennessee Beauty ended the season with a small, sweet berry.

With that many acres, it was only natural to open the fields to a "pick-your-own" patch. Sometimes people brought their children just to see how berries were grown. Of course, money could be saved if you picked your own. A quart was then 40 cents if it was filled level. But for those who liked to pile them up and run them over, the charge was 50 cents.

Dad liked to tease the customers. He told them it would be more profitable if we charged for the big, juicy berries they ate in the patch, instead of the ones in their baskets. This was a great family affair with Mom being the best strawberry picker of all.

Most people didn't realize that the best tasting berries were the small ones completely ripened by the sun. No sugar required!

A Fruitful Invention...

This fruit drier was patented in 1887 by Sylvester Stigler of Claysville.

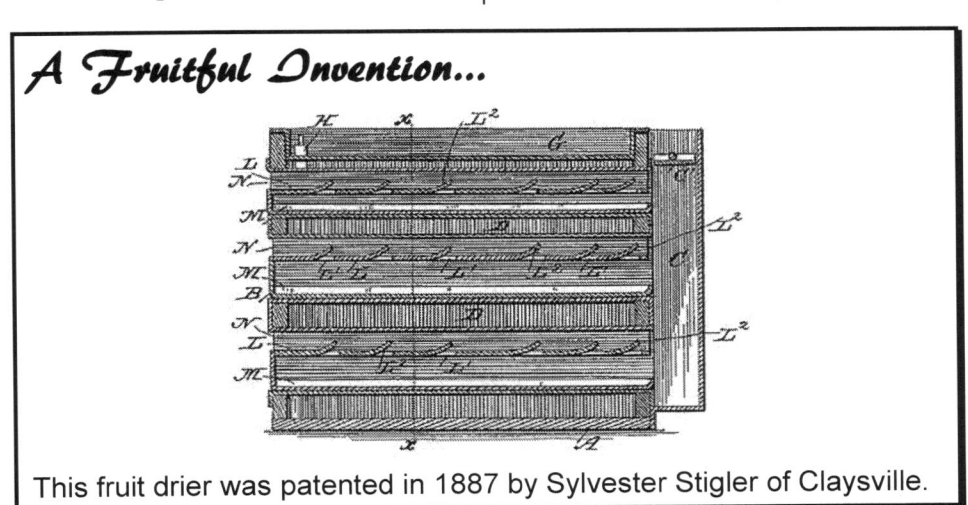

Grace Had a Little Lamb

BY MARK COOPER

Both kids and sheep grow up fast.

My mom, Grace, enjoyed sharing this story from her childhood. She loved helping her daddy, my Grandpa, care for his sheep. One day he told her something special was waiting in the sheep barn. Grace eagerly slipped inside, and found a new-born lamb shivering in a warm corner. Her daddy explained that the lamb's mother had refused to care for it. The lamb was very weak and wouldn't get better, unless someone chose to love it back to health. Was Grace willing to take on that challenge?

Of course she was! Every day she filled the lamb's bottle, careful not to spill any of the milk and formula. Then she'd nestle down in the straw, gather the weak lamb into her lap, and encourage him to suck from the bottle.

After a few days, the lamb's legs no longer wobbled, and he started bounding over to the gate to greet her. He still loved curling up in her lap to drink from his bottle.

But as he got stronger, Grace got sick. She had to stay in the house for several days. She worried about her little lamb. Would he be okay without her? After all, she was the one who had committed to loving him back to health. Her daddy assured her that although the lamb missed her, he was still eating and getting stronger.

Imagine her excitement

when her mother told her she could return to the barn. Although she still felt a bit weak and tired, she could hardly wait to feel the cuddly warmth of her lamb snuggling into her lap.

But when she entered the barn, Grace didn't see her little lamb. Rather she found a stocky and rambunctious young sheep, far too big to hold. With a puzzled look she turned to her daddy. He saw her confusion. "Grace," he said gently, "you took such good care of your lamb that he's growing into a big strong sheep." Her tears flowed as she realized she would never again hold her precious little lamb in her lap.

I imagine her daddy might have shed a tear or two of his own, watching his young daughter's tears flow, and knowing that she also was growing quickly and soon would think herself too big to curl up in his own lap.

Down on the Farm...

A young Gladys Gibson once had a lamb that grew to be a ram, circa 1935, in Jefferson Township where Salt Fork Lake is now.

Photo courtesy of Mrs. Gladys Gibson Zimmerman.

Hayin' by 'City Boys'

BY BOB LEY

Food for thought.

My friend, Jack, lived with his wife and two young sons on a farm a few miles east of Cambridge. A lot of the farm needed work, and though Jack was not speedy, he was gradually working on it.

One summer Jack became ill. It was time for the first cutting of hay. Hayin' time! There is a small window of time to get hay cut, dried, baled, and stored in the barns on consecutive dry days.

Farm folks stick together and help one another in time of need. Word went out that Jack needed help and two neighbors brought their tractors and cut the hay. A few days later, after some drying time, they were back with the tractors equipped to bale. Working all day, the men finished, leaving hundreds of bales strewn in their paths.

Several of Jack's friends from town, none of whom knew farming, were recruited to pick up the bales, load them on a flatbed trailer, then stack them in two of his barns. Jack suggested we wear long sleeve shirts and jeans. The forecast was 95 degrees, so a few of our gang showed up in tee shirts.

Fortunately, a couple of Jack's neighbors were there to direct us and to demonstrate how to stack the bales on the flatbed. Done correctly, huge numbers of bales would fit without falling over, saving a lot of time.

"Put the first bale on exactly like you plan on putting the last one," he warned. In other words, "Pace yourself."

After an hour, the men in tee shirts looked like they'd been playing with barbed wire. Hay is very prickly. One fellow managed to put his foot through a rotten floor board in the first barn, putting him out of commission. Then the elevator, a conveyor belt device used to take the bales from the ground to the loft, broke down. We were stuck heaving fifty-pound bales through the loft doors from below.

Finally done by supper time, we had a wiener roast and downed a few Iron Citys... known as "Arns" on the farms.

It was a tough day. My new awareness of what goes into farming made me respect it even more. The work was hard; the camaraderie was great. We "city boys" take a lot for granted. The experience made me appreciate just some of what farmers do for us!

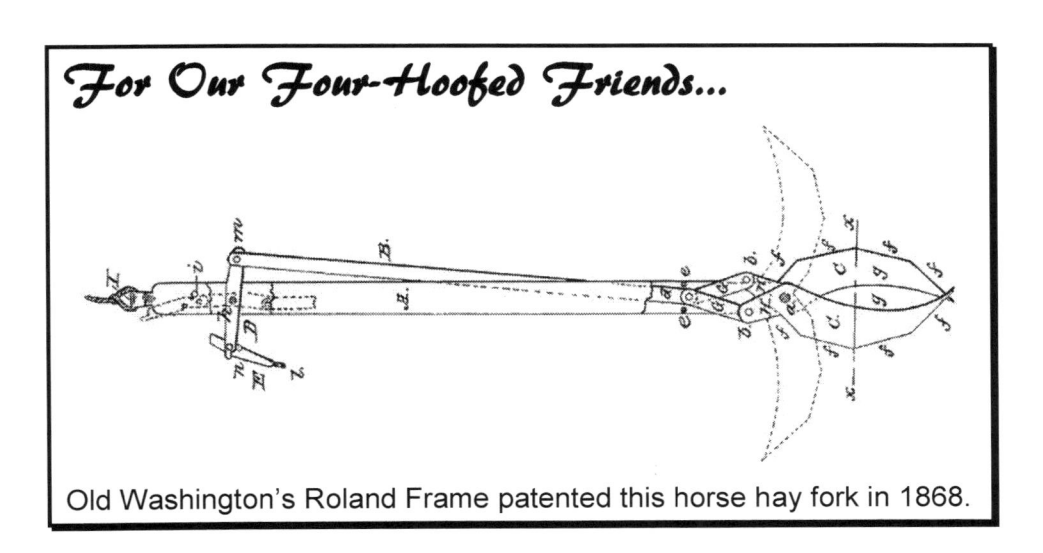

For Our Four-Hoofed Friends...

Old Washington's Roland Frame patented this horse hay fork in 1868.

Mom's Kitchen

BY JOY L. WILBERT ERSKINE

Dining in, in style.

Back in the old days, the 1960s, when my four siblings and I were growing up as military dependents, restaurant meals didn't happen very often. Dad's Air Force pay didn't allow for that kind of treat – well, maybe once in a great while. I do remember a few special occasions when we all went to Denny's or to a casino (we lived in Reno for a long while). Those were the best places to feed a crowd like ours without breaking the bank.

Most of the time, we dined at Mom's kitchen, where, right down to the little ones, we all had kitchen duties. Since I was the oldest, I helped Mom as assistant cook and head dishwasher. Jan set the table and dried dishes. Sherry, the youngest, helped Steve clear the table, while Ken was in charge of emptying out the trash. We were a well-trained military family team.

For as long as I can remember, a picnic table covered with a cheery red-and-white-checkered oilcloth served as a dinner table for us all. Bench seating afforded ample space to allow us to be able to eat meals as a family. Dinner was family time.

We ate very well, too. Meals were generally simple, but delicious and filling. I recall peeling lots of potatoes and Mom teaching me to make gravy from meat drippings. She excelled at making good, healthy meals from everyday ingredients. We often had Mexican food, because she had grown up on it in southern California. A meal of tacos, burritos, gorditas, or enchiladas, all of which we loved, provided an inexpensive, quick dinner for a family of seven.

Mom never skimped on dessert either. Ice cream could be purchased in five-gallon tubs at the commissary. We usually had two or three in the chest freezer in the garage, although sometimes the boys went through it pretty fast when no one was looking. Cookies, which it seemed Mom baked constantly, rarely made it from stove to table before sticky fingers nabbed them from the pans. She also liked to bake and decorate cakes, and taught us how to make homemade candy like fudge, divinity, and fondant.

Our family didn't miss eating out because meals at home were so dang good. Something tasty was always going on in Mom's Kitchen…and something wonderful was always happening around that cheery family picnic table.

Culinary Memories…

The author's "kitchen magician" mom, Marilyn (White) Wilbert, and Air Force dad, William "Bill" Wilbert.

My First Time Eating Out

BY MARK COOPER

A tale of fast food intimidation.

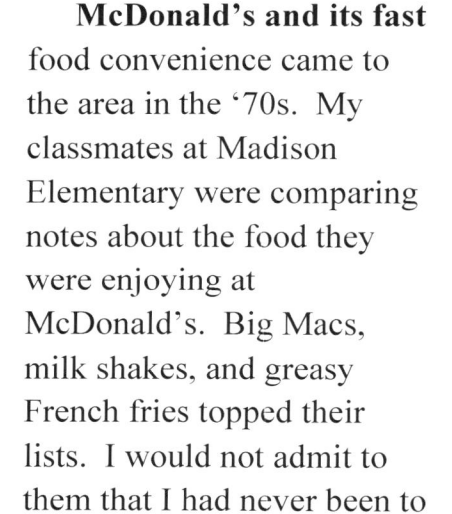

McDonald's and its fast food convenience came to the area in the '70s. My classmates at Madison Elementary were comparing notes about the food they were enjoying at McDonald's. Big Macs, milk shakes, and greasy French fries topped their lists. I would not admit to them that I had never been to *any* food establishment.

My parents considered eating out both impractical and unnecessary for their large family. The farm provided much of the food that showed up on the table at mealtimes. Mom canned and froze garden produce, and Dad fed out calves and pigs to be butchered at Patterson's Meat Market in Center. Mom and Dad figured our own "meat 'n potatoes" were tastier and less pricey than any restaurant could offer.

A school field trip introduced me to eating out. In previous years, our teachers instructed us to pack a sack lunch to eat while on our trips. But, for our fifth grade field trip to the Zane Gray Museum, we were told to bring lunch money because we would be eating at McDonald's.

I was excited, thinking about finally eating out. But I also recognized a problem – a problem so large that I was nervous for days beforehand. I didn't know how to order a meal. How would I keep from appearing a complete idiot in front of my classmates?

On that fateful day, we finished the museum tour and headed to McDonald's. As everyone else pushed through the doors, I hung back, happy for my classmates and teachers to cut in front of me. I watched my peers, hoping to learn enough to order my own food without having to ask for help. I saw food options were listed on an overhead menu screen and that the girl behind the counter was taking orders and money. The various meal deals and other choices seemed confusing.

As the line dwindled, my turn came to face the impatient teenaged cashier. Heart racing, palms sweating, and in a weak and shaky voice, I placed my order. The cashier had to ask me to repeat what I said. She ended up giving me food that wasn't quite what I'd ordered, but at least I had something to eat. Then all I had to worry about was how to fill my cup from the fountain machine, and what to do with my plastic tray when I was done eating.

That first experience at McDonald's may have served up more anxiety than enjoyment, but at least this farm boy could finally say he had eaten out.

Another Place to Eat...

Sailor Joe ran his "Hideaway" bar at the Coney Island restaurant in the 1950s. The old Coney Island became Theo's Restaurant today.

Photo courtesy of the Guernsey County History Museum.

Eateries

BY BOB LEY

What's fer dinner?

Walking around downtown Cambridge, beginning in the sixties, would reveal a plethora of eateries. I am going to recount as many as I can, and I invite you to join me!

The Point, a landmark for many years, later became the New River Grille, and is now known as the Point Tlaquepaque. Also gone are the Brass Grill, famous for Lew Wagner's cabbage rolls, and the Brass Rail, owned by Jim Toundas.

Across Wheeling Avenue was the Plaza, once owned by Mayor Sam Salupo. Bob Francis now owns Francis Family Restaurant there. Jake's Sandwich Shop and Gus Chelikis' Central Restaurant were a little further down the street.

Aggie's, owned by Aggie and Mabel Nickles, was a downtown favorite for many years. Later remodeled, it became the go-to place for fine dining under the name, The Gaslight. It is now the Downtown Arena. The Spot Café was located nearby, as well as Esper's Pizza.

The Yellow Front Saloon wasn't here long, but provided an eclectic place to eat. In the same block was the Cadillac Lounge, owned by Bill Nicolozakes.

The American Restaurant, run by Louis and Joe Jamail for 28 years, featured home-cooked family style meals.

The National Hotel, where the Jeff is now, boasted a small bar and dining room.

Ellis McCracken opened a popular cafeteria called the Kopper Kettle across from the Court House. Reuben's, a tiny lunch counter and bar, was across the street. Stone's Grill was a busy lunch-time eatery. Great pies, too!

Over on Steubenville Avenue was Galliher's. Yum stuff! The Guernsey Dairy Bar, run by Jim Siatris, featured great lunches and delicious ice cream treats.

Two of our three five-and-dime stores, S.S. Kresge and J.J. Newberry, included busy lunch counters. Farther down Wheeling Avenue, was Sally O'Sweets. Good food and even better candies!

The Coney Island, famous for their coney dogs, and partnered by Jim Granitsas and Nick Theodosopoulos, was later bought out by Nick. After a ruinous fire, the Theo family rebuilt it into a busy family restaurant called Theo's that is still a local attraction, famous for their pies!

The Berwick Hotel, like the National, offered a dining room and a bar famous for potent drinks!

Eid Francis had a restaurant on the hill on the north side of Wheeling Ave. Eid originated the "camel-rider sandwich."

George Jamiel's restaurant near the viaduct served as the breakfast headquarters for years. Do you remember the ribbon candy George made at Christmas?

A little farther out is John Lanning's Country Boy Restaurant. Mr. Savage had the first restaurant in that building. It was previously Taylors Meats.

Before Wally's, was East Village Pizza. First place I knew of to sell pizza by the slice.

Mr. Lee's uses "comfort food" as a specialty for those eating a little further out on

East Wheeling Avenue.

Also, Dog and Suds, A&W Root Beer, The Lodge, Burger Chef, the original House of Hunan (later re-opened near Riesbeck's), the L&K, and the Mecca Drive-In all did business here.

I have enjoyed our tour. I hope you did! If I missed a place, I apologize. Getting tougher and tougher to remember it all!

The Floor's the Same...

The Guernsey Dairy Lunch
THE PLACE TO EAT
Steaks and Chops at all hours
705 Wheeling Ave., CAMBRIDGE, OHIO

Today's McKenna's Market was the Guernsey Dairy Lunch in this 1910 picture. The tiled floor is still there!

Photo courtesy of the Guernsey County History Museum.

Bennett's Drive-In

BY BEVERLY WENCEK KERR

Shake, shake, shake.

Every Sunday our family hopped in the car and headed to Byesville to visit Mom's family. We would spend the day visiting Dede, Baba, aunts, uncles and cousins, who all lived within a block of each other in The Bottom.

A bit of excitement often happened on the way home when Dad would say, "Anyone want a milkshake?" Even Mom would smile and agree to the stop.

Most of you would think this wasn't a big deal, but we never ate at any restaurant or drive-in during my youth. Sure, we would eat with family at their homes sometimes or even at a church social, but not at a restaurant. Mom didn't think they were clean enough, as she was a champion when it came to keeping things perfectly clean in the kitchen and the house.

But for some reason, she felt Bennett's Drive-In was an acceptable place to get a hot dog and milkshake, which was our usual order whenever we stopped. Dad's favorite milkshake was cherry, mine chocolate, and Mom's vanilla.

This wonderful little ice cream stand was located on Route 21, just at the edge of Cambridge. Owners, Jack and June Bennett, made their own ice cream there beginning in 1951, and it tasted extra good. Another specialty was their wonderful sloppy joe sandwich, made from a special family recipe. Rumor has it that recipe was recently shared with Parkside Tasty Treat at the Cambridge City Park.

Route 21 was the perfect location for an ice cream stand in 1951, as it was the only route at that time from Marietta to Cleveland. There were no interstates, so everyone going north or south passed by this little ice cream stand and business was good.

Jack worked full time at the State Hospital, where he was in charge of the kitchen. That meant that June ran the ice cream stand during the day. When Jack came home at 4:30, June fixed supper for the family and Jack ran the stand until closing. On the weekends both of them worked there, but the children seldom, if ever, worked the counter.

Perhaps Jack and June knew how hard they had worked and hoped that their children would have an easier life someday. My parents were very much the same when I was a child, not wanting me to work around the farm, as they explained, "You'll have to work hard when you get older, so enjoy life now."

But the Bennett boys did do little things to help, like mop the floors or pick up papers in the parking lot. Sometimes they might even find a nickel or dime that someone dropped on their way to the car. A coin could be important at that time when ice cream was only seven cents a scoop. Imagine getting a three-scoop cone for twenty-one cents!

Those stops at Bennett's Drive-In were always anticipated the moment we left my grandparents' home in Byesville. Dad usually wouldn't mention it until we got to Cambridge. Then he'd casually say, "Let's stop by and get a milkshake." Mom and I always agreed.

Even today, it only seems natural that if I get a milkshake, a hot dog should be included in the order. Anyone for a milkshake and hot dog? 〰️RD❧〰️

Speaking of Drive-Ons...

"DIZZYLAND"

Opens Tonight

SUNDAY—2 PM TILL 9 PM

ALL RIDES ONLY 10¢

The old Cruise-In drive-in theatre was just west of Cambridge on the north side of Route 40 where the Pritchard-Laughlin Civic Center stands today. In 1958, kids could enjoy their "Dizzyland" rides for just 10¢!

Photo courtesy of the Guernsey County History Museum.

My Aunt Margaret McBride

BY HARRIETTE MCBRIDE ORR

Life on a higher level.

Excitement always built when I heard Dad say, "Sis is coming home." His sister, Margaret, attended Muskingum College, graduated from Ohio University, and obtained her Master's degree from Case Western Reserve University. She did student teaching in the one room schools of Guernsey County, including the small town of "Dog Town." Upon graduation she landed a job in Minerva, Ohio, where she taught for three years.

To my grandparents' dismay, Aunt Margaret hired a headhunter to find her a job teaching in Euclid, a suburb of Cleveland, Ohio. In 1941 she started her career at Euclid's Shore, a school of two thousand, with classes from kindergarten through grade twelve. When World War II broke out, she felt called to serve her country and enlisted in the Women's Army Corps. She hoped to see the world, but was stationed for most of the time in the Boston area. When the war ended she was just completing her overseas training at Camp Crowder, Missouri. Disappointed that she never got to leave the United States, she was very proud of her service to her country. She mustered out as a Chief Leader, equivalent to a Master Sergeant.

Aunt Margaret returned to teaching in Euclid, because she considered developing a world outlook in children as a first step to world peace. It was her hope that her students would grow into humane, intelligent adults, who would work for the brotherhood of all mankind.

Any time Aunt Margaret came home to Cambridge, I got to stay with her, at Grandma and Grandpa's. Time spent with her was such a joy. During the day she shared her love of baking cookies and trying new recipes, or ice skating on a nearby pond. Bath time was special because we had no bathtub at home. She used Apple Blossom bubble bath and Yardley's English lavender soap. She taught me to make beds the "Army way" and how to set my hair in pin curls, using bobby pins and a head band, to create a "pageboy style."

Our bedroom was upstairs where there was no heat, so she warmed the bed with a hot water bottle. We slept between layers of a double blanket, with comforters piled on top. Before turning out the light, and saying our prayers, she always read to me from the small library of books from her childhood, or the latest scholastic "Reading Circle Book."

Aunt Margaret was always teaching, and to a child she was such an interesting person. Always up on the latest styles and fads of the day, one Christmas she came home, with her blonde hair styled in a Mamie Eisenhower hairdo, with the famous bangs the President's wife always sported.

Miss Manners would have loved her. She sent the family books on etiquette, and expected us to use them to guide our lives.

Always well-groomed, she kept her body in trim shape. She never learned to drive so she walked a great deal. Always prepared, she never left the house without hat and gloves, as well as a satchel containing rain hats, umbrella, plastic rain coat and overshoes.

She continually exposed our family to the arts, history, and current events. If there was a museum nearby, we had to visit. My reading was encouraged by a box of books that arrived every month. My mother had to hide them so I would get my work done, but I often found her reading them too.

Late at night Aunt Margaret could be found writing letters to family and friends, keeping us all in touch. Cards were sent for every occasion and if you were ill, cards came several times a week. She created Sunshine Boxes for her shut-in friends. These were boxes filled with small wrapped gifts, one to be opened each day.

Aunt Margaret was a most generous person who could never do enough for those she cared for. All that was expected in return was a thank you. Her standards were high and she always went the extra mile to make anything she did special. She taught her nieces and nephews to do the same. Her mantra was, "With a little effort, life can be lived on a higher level." This she did with gusto.

Career Planning...

| Muskingum College is the Place for Ambitious and Worthy Young Men and Women |

The ad at left was placed in the 1913 Cambridge High School yearbook.

Brain vs. Calculator

BY MARTHA F. JAMAIL

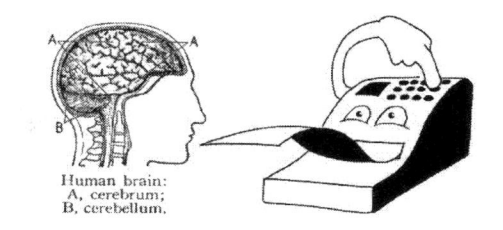

Brain power doesn't require batteries.

Just so you know before you read any further, I think the brain beats calculator every time – at least in the fundamentals of 4th grade multiplication facts.

It just happened to be an ordinary day in my 4th grade classroom at Park Elementary School. Math was usually the first subject I instructed in the morning, when students' minds were the sharpest.

We had been trying to master the basic 100 multiplication facts, and there was a practice sheet we used each morning. The students only had to read the numbers (e.g. 6 x 3) and write the answer – 18. The lessons were timed (only three minutes allowed), and they were to stop immediately when the timer rang. We traded papers for scoring and the students recorded the number correct. No matter what the score was, they were encouraged to get a higher score the next day. The goal was for everyone to master the 100 facts.

As with all children, some are better at memorization than others, but one day I had an unexpected assist in proving its importance. A box of new calculators arrived for our class, and everyone was excited. One of the students blurted out, "Hey, now we don't have to memorize those multiplication facts. We can do them with our new calculators!"

I decided right then was a good time to show the power of memorization. There were already a few students who could complete the sheet in less than 3 minutes, so I asked for a volunteer.

I made a transparency of the worksheet and placed it on the overhead projector for the whole class to see. Then I asked the student who favored the calculator if he would like to compete with the volunteer. He eagerly answered, "Sure!"

The timer was set and they both began. The student completing the problems on the overhead projector was finished long before the timer rang, and long before the calculator-assisted student. They were good sports about it, and eventually the entire class mastered the fact sheet in less than three minutes.

Score one for the brain!

≈RDW≈

Think Fast...

6 X 7 =	5 X 9 =	5 X 4 =	8 X 0 =	10 X 3 =
9 X 5 =	4 X 4 =	4 X 6 =	1 X 7 =	0 X 4 =
2 X 9 =	1 X 10 =	9 X 10 =	4 X 2 =	6 X 8 =
4 X 9 =	7 X 5 =	2 X 3 =	6 X 1 =	10 X 10 =
0 X 5 =	6 X 1 =	6 X 0 =	0 X 2 =	1 X 1 =
5 X 5 =	8 X 7 =	4 X 6 =	7 X 8 =	9 X 7 =
9 X 8 =	6 X 2 =	6 X 3 =	6 X 5 =	2 X 1 =
10 X 6 =	9 X 6 =	10 X 5 =	8 X 4 =	5 X 7 =
7 X 4 =	5 X 3 =	3 X 3 =	5 X 4 =	2 X 5 =
4 X 5 =	2 X 7 =	3 X 0 =	3 X 1 =	1 X 4 =
5 X 9 =	2 X 3 =	3 X 1 =	8 X 10 =	6 X 0 =
7 X 9 =	10 X 5 =	4 X 5 =	7 X 6 =	9 X 10 =

Oh, the terror of the timed "times table" tests of fourth grade! In just one or two unforgiving minutes, the goal was usually to get a perfect score. Try this speed challenge against a kid with a calculator!

What I Learned

BY BOB LEY

Mom the School Marm.

I had several talented teachers who tolerated my behavior and taught me readin', writin', and 'rithmetic, as well as what it means to be a gentleman. A product of a Catholic school education in the fifties, I can recount many 'nun tales' that shaped my life for the better. The teacher who taught me the most, however, was not one I had in school.

My wife, Sue, had completed two years at Ohio University prior to our marriage. Being a stay-at-home mother for several years was enjoyable, but when college loomed for our three children, she went to work as a teacher's aide.

After ten years as an aide, we decided it was time she should finish her education and become an elementary teacher. Going back to college was exciting for her. She tackled it with a vengeance. It took four years going part-time. They went by like a whirlwind. School went well and being in her forties was an advantage to her. Because she was older than some of her teachers, her age helped in getting respect. She wasn't of an age to party with the younger students, many of whom thought of her as a mother figure.

Meanwhile, I was learning, too. Things like grocery shopping, laundry, packing lunches, going to dance recitals, and cleaning house. I was already fairly well experienced in cooking and ironing clothes! (Thanks, Mom!) Everyone survived it. Her graduation was a day of immense pride for me. Sue got her degree and was hired into the Cambridge School District.

Most teachers are dedicated. I think Sue's experience as an aide, having raised three children, and her enthusiasm for children, all before she started to teach, heightened her success. Always caring, I have seen her have zippers replaced in winter coats for children who had little. I have watched her prepare and deliver lesson plans to parents as guides for them to help a struggling child. Sue loved to teach and loved her kids. She wanted each one to have that thirst for learning that makes a successful adult. Sue wanted to improve their lives forever.

From her I learned the value of dedication, of creating order out of chaos, the advantages of teamwork, and what giving willingly means.

An Artist's Conception...

On October 18th, 1959, Cambridge's new high school on Clairmont Avenue was dedicated. This image was on the event program's cover. Cecil McFarland was this high school's first principal.

Photo courtesy of the Guernsey County History Museum.

My Kindergarten Report Card

BY MARK COOPER

Subject mastery took some time.

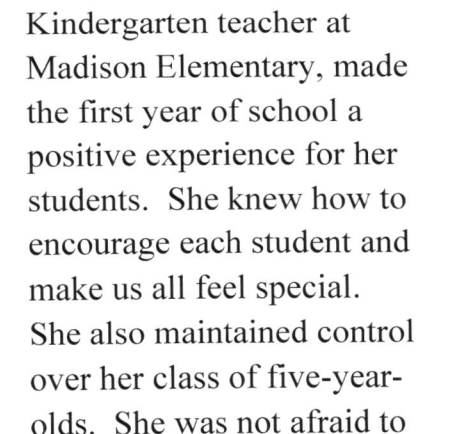

    Mrs. Whitmer, my Kindergarten teacher at Madison Elementary, made the first year of school a positive experience for her students. She knew how to encourage each student and make us all feel special. She also maintained control over her class of five-year-olds. She was not afraid to employ the dreaded, "Class! Put your heads down on your desks!" discipline technique.

    After my mom passed away, I was sorting through numerous papers she had kept. To my surprise, I found my Kindergarten report card, now more than 30 years old. Looking it over, I saw that we were evaluated in categories such as how we got along with others, our communication skills, and even our ability to put on and fasten our coats without assistance. Each category had three options: "Does well," "Satisfactory," and "Needs Improvement."

    According to Mrs. Whitmer, I got along well with my classmates. She also noted my communication skills were satisfactory, which may have been her gentle way of saying, "He talks too much." I was feeling pretty good about my report card until I reached, "Puts on and fastens coat." A big red circle and bold red letters proclaimed,

"Needs Improvement." Ouch!

A few months after finding the report card, I spotted my former teacher and her husband at the Guernsey County Farmer's Market. Grinning, I slipped up beside her, "Mrs. Whitmer, I can put on my coat now."

She smiled. Her response was short and succinct, "Well I'm glad!"

The Pride of Steubenville Avenue...

Union High School once stood at the northeast corner of Steubenville Avenue and 7th Street in Cambridge. Students first arrived in 1874.

Photo courtesy of the Guernsey County History Museum.

Remembering Andre Odebrecht

BY RICK BOOTH

Teaching math across the generations.

"Andre Odebrecht is only going to teach math for one more year before he retires," my father explained to me one day. He'd somehow heard the news through the grapevine. "He's an excellent teacher. I learned a lot in his classes. I think you should try to take both third and fourth year math from him next year." This was the challenge Dad laid before me in the spring of 1972.

My father had gone through Cambridge High School in the 1940s. He then went on to major in physics at Ohio State before spending three years in the Navy and then seeking a law degree. Over the years, he was always teaching me mathematical principles ahead of my grade level, so I give him much of the credit for my knack for numbers that resulted in good test marks at school. Long before I got to high school, though, I'd heard of one math teacher in particular whom he really admired – Andre Odebrecht. Mr. Odebrecht had been a young man when Dad took his courses in school, and he occasionally commented that he was looking forward to my taking similar courses from him a generation later.

As I recall him, Mr. Odebrecht was not a particularly tall man. Neither was he thin, though I wouldn't say he was fat. He was solid and balding, but not entirely bald. There was a certain notable roundness of face and head. His voice was somewhat high-pitched, and he spoke rapidly, which gave a sense of urgency to anything he said, even if nothing was urgent. He was old school – formal both in dress and mannerisms. For much of his career, he also held a night job as a railroad telegrapher. Though usually mild-mannered, Mr. Odebrecht did have a temper that sometimes flared when a question he posed to a student was met with a deer-in-the-headlights response. His nickname among students was "The Ode."

Thanks to Dad, I was pretty well prepared to take both junior and senior math courses from Andre Odebrecht during my junior year of high school. Dad felt the quality of Mr. Odebrecht's teaching would serve me well in later years, as it had for him. The subject matter of the senior year was not closely dependent on the junior year material, so taking both courses at once was doable. I think I was the only student Mr. Odebrecht ever had who took both years of math from him at once. As a teacher, he wasn't warm and fuzzy, but he was good, and he was fair. Dad was right.

I pretty much aced both courses that year, though it took a fair amount of work. I also made quite a few friends by re-explaining lessons and problem-solving techniques to others who found the material challenging. I liked many of the teachers I had in high school, but Andre Odebrecht stood out as the most memorable. That's how my father felt about him, too. I'm still pretty good at math, and am glad to give much of the credit to the teacher once named by his students – with a mix of awe, fear, and reverence – the Ode.

Then and Now...

Cambridge became a maintenance hub for the Cleveland & Marietta Railroad – later part of the Pennsylvania Railroad – in the 1870s. Above, 37 men pose on the roundhouse turntable, circa 1930. Below, the turntable's remains lying next to the county jail, 1995.

Photos courtesy of the Guernsey County History Museum, Adair Collection

Sprechen Sie Deutsch?

BY JOY L. WILBERT ERSKINE

I suspect I was the "entertainment."

From 1965 to 1968, I studied German under the tutelage of two intense, but wonderful, German teachers, Herr Asmus and Frau Lichter; he in Reno, Nevada, and she in Bitburg, Germany. My ancestry on my father's side comes from Germany, so my choice of foreign language was a natural one. It was a good decision because, during my father's brief assignment to France before Charles DeGaulle kicked the Americans and Canadians out in 1966, I attended school there and discovered that I was terrible at French. But France wasn't a total loss because I learned how to kiss. (Another story… maybe… someday.)

Both Herr Asmus and Frau Lichter were tall and thin, almost skeletal, with strong, angular faces. They wore perpetual, stern, unforgiving expressions that made you pay attention for fear of getting into trouble. It's a deceiving German characteristic, because I learned pretty quickly that no matter who you talk to, if you make the effort to communicate in German, the harsh façade quickly dissipates and they become very cordial and helpful— and they will reciprocate by speaking English! It could be that they cultivate the intimidating demeanor in order to command the upper hand – definitely a good strategy with teenagers.

German came easy to me at 14 and 15. I looked forward to class every day, even when the lessons were difficult, because these two teachers brought out my best. They had confidence in me, so it was easier to have confidence in myself. Before long, I was not only speaking German fairly well, I was *thinking* in German too. That was a fun experience!

Living in Germany for three years during that time of my life was very helpful as I learned the language and used it every day. Translating for my parents, although my efforts were rudimentary, was a skill builder for me and bolstered my self-assurance. The people I practiced on were kind, seeming to appreciate my efforts in spite of my obvious mistakes, and my practical and social skills increased as well. The opportunity was priceless.

Years later, as a wife and mother, I became the translator for my family again when we rented the upstairs apartment of a particularly charming German home surrounded by white picket fencing and rose bushes. Our landlord and his wife, both confined to wheelchairs, were avid rose gardeners. For entertainment on weekends, they often invited friends, including us, to join them on their back patio for an impromptu party. I suspect I was the "entertainment" part of those evenings. They spoke no English and my German was rusty, but there were smiles and laughter all around, and with the encouragement of a little Parkbräu Pirminator, we actually seemed to communicate quite well.

My German skills are now a distant memory. Too many years have passed, and I have little opportunity to speak the language. However, I've started brushing up with a language app, just for fun. I'm beginning to think in German a little bit again. As I practice, the faces of these two favorite teachers reappear in my mind's eye. They seem to be watching over my efforts—and they're smiling. Ja, Herr Asmus und Frau Lichter, ich spreche wieder Deutsch, ein bisschen. Danke!

Danke schön...

Thanks to Frau Helene Lichter, at least one of the Rainy Day Writers can speak, read, and write German. Watch out, Goethe!

High School Journalism

BY BEVERLY WENCEK KERR

Planting seeds of creativity.

Creative writing was a weekly feature of Hazel McCulley's journalism class during my senior year at Cambridge High School. Nearly every Friday a story was due from a given topic. Most gave plenty of room for creativity.

One assignment still sticks in my mind. "The Life of a Stick of Gum" produced some interesting stories. You'd be surprised at the uses it might have and the places it might venture.

The goal of the journalism class was to prepare students to write articles creatively, then make practical use of this knowledge by writing articles for publication.

Therefore, each week our class produced the J-G page, which appeared in The Daily Jeffersonian. As Junior Grade reporters, we were given free rein to create a full page in our local newspaper to summarize high school news. We reported on school activities, highlighted outstanding students, and wrote editorials concerning school issues.

As part of this class, we took a field trip to the Jeffersonian to see how various departments operated. We saw the composing room with reporters typing their articles, and also watched the typesetter as he set print for the page that we were creating. No computer-driven technology existed at that time.

Miss McCulley encouraged us on every task. She made us believe we could write about anything. Her goal was to prepare us to write better for college classes in the future.

Serious about her role as an educator, she required students to give their best. At the same time, Miss McCulley showed interest in each student and their dreams. Students never doubted who was in charge, but she conducted the class with a sweet disposition.

Even her appearance demanded respect. This tall lady wore her light brown hair pulled back into a bun. Always dressed professionally in a suit or fashionable dress, her Lily of the Valley scent followed her down the rows of desks. You wouldn't even think of arguing with anything she said because of her pleasant manner.

When correcting or critiquing papers, she never used red ink. Her choice of a more soothing green ink didn't seem as harsh. In years to come, red ink was never my choice for correcting papers either. It seemed an angry color.

Perhaps her clever way of presenting writing influenced my choice of writing as a hobby today. Thanks for all the encouragement given by teachers along the way, especially Miss Hazel McCulley.

Before Word Processors...

High school journalism used to mean plenty of time spent at a typewriter. The 1959 Cambridge High School typing room, at left, was once a noisy place.

My Favorite Teachers

BY MARTHA F. JAMAIL

The impact of good teachers is immeasurable.

> Sister Mary Annette
> Sister Marie Catherine
> Sister Norbert Mary
> Sister Ruth Virginia

Their names read like a Litany of the Saints – those Catholic nuns who were my elementary school teachers. Along with my parents, these dedicated professionals helped form my early education, my Catholic faith, and my belief in God. My teachers belonged to the Order of Sisters of Charity from Nazareth, Kentucky, and taught at St. Elizabeth Parochial School in Clarksdale, Mississippi.

Unfortunately, the humid heat of the southern Delta was not kind to the nuns, who were required to wear the habit of their order. It consisted of a full length, long-sleeved black dress, with a short, elbow-length black cape, black hose, and black lace-up shoes. The only color relief was a white collar, and a starched white bonnet as a head covering.

Needless to say, we students never complained about the heat in front of the Sisters. There was no air conditioning in our school, only open windows, and a ceiling fan that seemed to have just one setting – slow.

Sister Mary Annette was the most jovial of all the

nuns, always smiling and laughing. As a child I actually thought her name was Sister "Merry" Annette because of her happy demeanor. She was my kindergarten teacher, and later, my first and second grade teacher.

One day I decided to bring flowers to Sister. My mother was fond of daffodils, so our backyard flowerbeds were overflowing with them. I went out back before school, and began picking flowers until there were more than I could hold, so I put them in a bucket, and continued picking. By the time Mom saw me, the bucket was full! She just laughed and managed to band the flowers together with aluminum foil, and soon we were on our way.

I remember thinking that no one had ever given Sister so many flowers, and how happy she would be. When I walked into the classroom, she thanked me and said she knew just what to do with them. Then she promptly placed them on the back table, and started our morning routine.

When our class returned from the first recess break, my flowers were gone. I was very disappointed, but just curious enough to go up and ask Sister where the flowers were. She whispered in my ear where she had put them, and said I could go see them at the next recess.

After hurrying through my lunch, I walked over to the adjoining convent, where the nuns lived. The entry door on the side opened to the chapel. When I walked inside, I was surprised to see all my bright yellow daffodils had been placed in several vases on the altar. It was beautiful! From Sister Mary Annette I learned to find the joy in life and learning.

All the classrooms at St.

Elizabeth were made up of combined grades: 1-2, 3-4, 5-6, and 7-8. It was actually beneficial because the younger students got a preview of expectations at the next level, and the older students got a basic review of what they had previously learned. Students participated during their instruction, and worked quietly on their assignments while the other class was being taught.

Sister Marie Catherine, my teacher for 3rd and 4th grade, was petite and short in stature. Actually, she wasn't much taller than her students. On the first day of school I remember telling my mother that Sister looked so cute, I wanted to hug her. You can imagine my embarrassment when Mother told Sister what I had said. It was quite a pleasant surprise when Sister responded by giving me a big, welcoming hug.

Cursive writing was first taught in third grade and my classmates and I were excited to be able to use pens for the first time – the new ink-flowing ballpoint pens. Sister instructed us to write using the Palmer Method, which required lots of practice. Each day we used the functionally shaped pens to make continuous overlapping circles across our lined notebook paper. The next line was made up of continuous up and down strokes with the pen touching the top and bottom of the lines across our paper. We alternated the circles with up and down strokes throughout the page, until the finished product looked like a series of thunderstorms. Sister's guidance and all the practice worked, because my cursive writing still earns compliments today. (Of course, any cursive writing found in the future will unfortunately be the new hieroglyphics, because cursive writing is no longer taught in school.)

Third and fourth grades were memorable because of Sister's classroom library that included many fairy tales and several "How to Draw" books. I read them all, and later used many of them with my own students during my teaching career.

Sister also gave us many opportunities to stand before the class to give book reports or to tell a story. There was a set time limit for our stories, and one day I had definitely run over my allotted time. Sister gently reminded me to wind it up, but amazingly, the students spoke out, "Please, Sister, let her finish. We like her story!" I can still remember my excitement in realizing the class was enjoying my made-up story, and Sister graciously granted me an extension. After adding a few more thoughts to end the story, I thanked Sister and went to my seat. (I learned that day it's a good thing to leave your audience wanting more.)

Sister Norbert Mary was the music teacher who taught choir as well as musical instruments. My family signed me up for piano lessons in the third grade. Sister was an excellent music teacher and also demonstrated a good sense of humor about how nuns are perceived.

One day, during one of my piano lessons in the convent music room, I noticed a framed photo of a woman had been placed on the piano. I asked Sister who it was, and she said the lady was her mother. Before giving it any thought, I blurted out, "You have a mother?" and Sister just dissolved in peals of laughter. When she finally gained control she asked, "Martha, did you think I just came down from heaven dressed like this?" Honestly, I don't know what I was thinking at the time, but most of us students did place the nuns on a pedestal of sorts. Sister left the room and returned shortly with a small photo album, and patiently showed me pictures of her entire family. It was a life lesson I'll always remember…but the piano lessons were soon forgotten. I was not meant to play the piano. Under Sister's careful direction though, the choir lessons were joyful for all of us. She made us proficient in singing hymns in Latin as well as English.

Sister Ruth Virginia was my fifth and sixth grade teacher, and amazingly, she requested to be our teacher for seventh and eighth grade too. Actually, what made her such a remarkable teacher was that she made every one of us students feel important, that she genuinely cared for us, and wanted us to succeed to the best of our ability. She is the main reason I wanted to become a teacher, an artist, and why I enjoy books. She read to us every day – even when we were seventh and eighth graders.

Sister had a unique way of making each and every one of her students feel special, even when we were being corrected. For example, I had been arriving late for school at least once a week – not by much, but at least 5 to 10 minutes each time. Instead of scolding me, Sister would sing, "A dillar, a dollar, here comes my 10 o'clock scholar." I laughed, the class laughed with me, and soon I was no longer arriving late.

Spelling bees, which started in grade 3, were continued throughout fifth and sixth grades, and in addition to our studies, Sister added another classroom activity – walking with good posture. She would have each of us balance a book on our head and with shoulders back, walk the perimeter of the classroom while music played. We all enjoyed it, especially since it was a competition. If your book fell, you returned to your seat until only one student remained. Sister always encouraged everyone to do their best. Soon we were all able to balance our book through the entire song.

Sister Ruth Virginia was that special teacher who also looked for hidden talents that each of us possessed. When she discovered it, she'd provide a venue for you to use it. She also had great empathy for her students. There was one student in our class who found it difficult to sit for long periods of time, so instead of scolding him, Sister gave him many opportunities to deliver messages to different classrooms, in addition to taking the daily lunch count to the office. He was also the only handicapped student in the room – he used crutches. Gerald never felt handicapped because of Sister's genius.

It was during 7th and 8th grade that Elvis Presley first became popular, and one day a student brought his 45 record to class for everyone to hear. The rock and roll music was infectious, and since it was recess, Sister let us move our desks to the corner so we could dance. She was definitely unique and wanted us proficient in every way – including socially. We all realized what a special time we had during our last four years with Sister, when upon graduation she read to us her predictions for each of us for the future. She predicted very well for many of us. I wish my favorite teachers were still around, so I could tell them how amazing they were and how much I appreciated their impact on my life.

A Tale of Two Churches...
ST. BENEDICTS CATHOLIC CHURCH AND SCHOOL

St. Benedict's Catholic Church has had two incarnations in Cambridge. The small church shown at left, near the present church location, was dedicated on December 12, 1897. At that time, the stated plan was to build a much larger church for a growing population on the same property within a few years. By 1910, finishing touches were being put on the St. Benedict's we know today.

ST. BENEDICT'S CATHOLIC

Photos courtesy of the Guernsey County History Museum.

A Writer's Inspiration

BY BETSY TAYLOR

On the edge of my seat.

In many cases, a writer can identify a pivotal event that guides her toward the writing endeavor. My event came when I was in second grade at the old Ninth Street School in Cambridge. The class had just finished a workbook exercise when our teacher, Mrs. Thomas, announced a special visitor. An elderly Indian woman, who was visiting relatives at Muskingum College, had come to tell us about her country.

Today I know that "exotic" is the perfect word to describe the lady. Her long, deep red, wrap-around dress, called a sari, was enhanced by gold embroidery. Bracelets jangled on her wrists as she moved gracefully in front of the blackboard backdrop. A red dot adorned her forehead just above her nose. She wore her long gray hair pulled into a bun on the back of her head. Most of the older ladies I knew wore their hair in short curly styles. Only kids had long hair that could be worn in braids or ponytails.

Mrs. Thomas invited us to ask questions about India as a country and about Indian customs. Then she turned the presentation over to our guest. When our guest spoke, I was captivated. Her English was perfect, but she had a pleasant accent that drew us to pay close attention. I don't remember the questions that were asked or the answers given, but I remember vividly the story she told.

The tale, she said, was Indian folklore about a brave little boy who lived in a small village near a dense jungle. The village sat in a clearing where crops were grown. The soft cadence of her words, along with the afternoon warmth, relaxed us as our eyes followed her gestures and the gentle sway of her sari.

She told us that the village was not as idyllic as it appeared in daylight, because livestock had begun to disappear during the night. Each morning, men from the village discovered tiger tracks near the animal enclosures. The tracks told the men that the creature was a very large tiger, a powerful beast.

The villagers set traps around their livestock pens and at the edge of the jungle, then waited fearfully for the tiger to be caught. At sunset each evening, the humans closed themselves indoors and ceded the dark to the tiger. At first, guards were posted, but they were armed only with rakes and hoes. The horrible roars that seemed to come from every direction soon convinced them that being out after dark was inviting death.

As the storyteller drew us in, the classroom disappeared and I could see myself huddled in a tiny house listening to the tiger roar, and watching the fearful faces of my family.

At one point in the story, the boy was compelled to step into the jungle. He was certain it was safe because the tiger had only hunted at night, and the afternoon was bright.

As he became lost in his task, he was lulled by the heat and the drone of insects. Our visitor had lulled us, too. Her voice had sweetened and softened, so that, when she suddenly clawed her hands, leaned forward, and lowered her voice menacingly, she shocked us with, "There was the tiger!"

At the word "tiger," the whole class jumped in their seats. As if it were only five minutes ago, I remember my heart leaping in my chest and my body's reaction to its "start reflex." I actually saw the tiger.

The boy overcame his paralyzing terror and raced for the village. Behind him, the tiger bounded after its next meal. Did the child know he was leading the huge cat toward a tiger trap? The storyteller didn't reveal that – only the crashing tumble the animal took into the concealed pit as the boy ran along its rim.

Now I know that the tiger's appearance in the jungle is the story's climax, and the boy's celebration as the hero is the denouement. But, as I listened to Mrs. Thomas chuckle and congratulate our visitor over her ability to "make every kid in the classroom jump in his seat," I wasn't thinking about story construction. My only reaction was, "That was great! I want to do that."

At Cambridge Junior High, I learned to follow writing rules. I could construct sentences and arrange them into paragraphs. Topic sentences, as my guides, were generally placed first in paragraphs. I loved rules that I could follow to produce a product, but I always admired that stuff called creativity and feared I didn't have it.

During my Cambridge High School years, I became proficient in a technical sense. I earned good grades and won several essay contests. The scholarships I earned were based, in part, on my communication skills. I respect those skills, but I still yearn to be a storyteller.

I still want to make kids | jump in their seats.

A Man of Design...

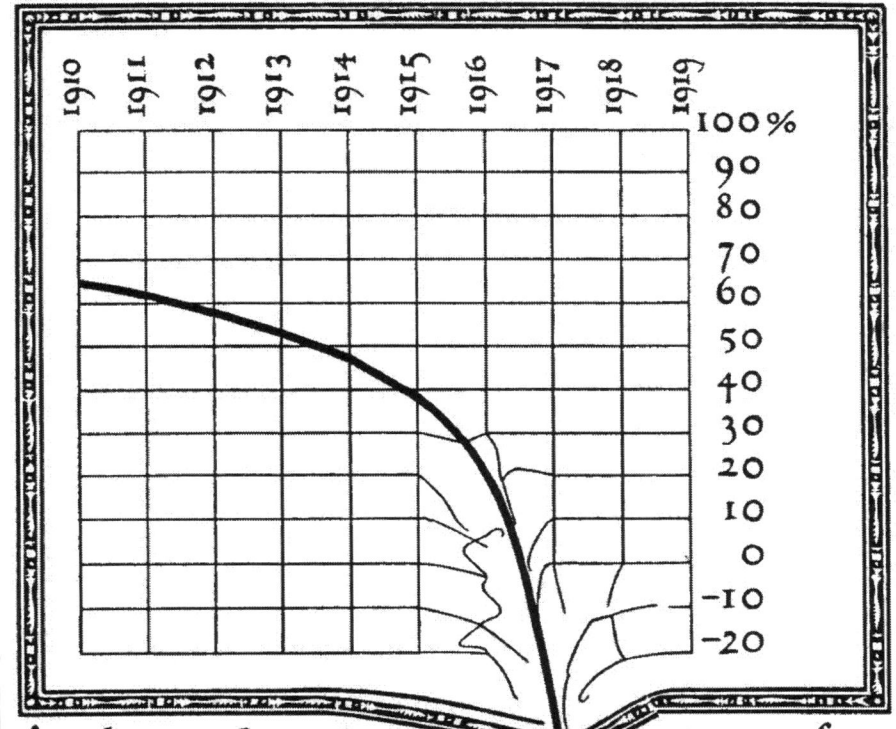

A chart showing the percentage of excellence in the physical properties of books published since 1910.

William A. "Bill" Dwiggins grew up in Cambridge and went on to become one of the most celebrated "graphic designers" of typefaces and books in the early twentieth century. In fact, he invented the term "graphic designer." He felt that books and their contents deserved to be created with great attention to artistic and stylistic detail. Cheap book production for the mass market in the early 1900s distressed his sensibilities. This chart shows his dismay at sinking standards.

Similarities of the Past

BY SAMUEL D. BESKET

Round and round it goes. Where it stops, nobody knows.

"What has been, will be again, what has been done, will be done again; there is nothing new under the sun."
– Ecclesiastes 1:9

My father used this scripture verse many times. So, is anything new or has it existed for ages in a different form? Is it a new idea or an echo from the past? Even computers, which we consider a new invention, existed in ancient Chinese cultures, only in a different form. So, is it really new, or has it happened before and is now manifested differently?

Here are a few examples:

Texting: It's the latest craze in communication, and everyone is doing it, even our president. But is texting only a modern version of the telegraph? As a ten-year-old boy, I loved going to the B&O depot in Lore City to watch the telegrapher as he copied and tapped out messages to faraway places.

Amazon: Amazon is one of the largest on-line shopping websites in the world. Simply find what you want, confirm your method of payment, and the item arrives at your door a few days later. The Sears & Roebuck catalogue operated on the same principle; it just took a little longer to receive the merchandise. My mother looked forward to the arrival of the seasonal catalogues. The Christmas edition was the favorite for my brothers and me.

Strip Malls: Shopping malls were the craze of the '70s. They sprang up around the outskirts of cities and destroyed the downtown business districts. Strip malls, or a new version of our downtown business districts, are the latest trend. Simply park in front of the store of your preference and avoid the hassle of trudging up and down the mall with an armful of packages. Sound familiar?

Freeze Dried: Freeze-drying is a dehydration process used to preserve perishable material to make it easy to store and transport. It is widely used in industry, particularly the food industry. Simply put, it's a process that removes water from a material by allowing it to slowly evaporate. I first became aware of freeze-drying when my mother did the laundry in the winter. She would hang the wet clothes outside and they would slowly freeze. After an hour or two, she would bring them into the house, where they would thaw out and slowly crumple to the floor, a little damp, but relatively dry.

Dollar Stores: Dollar Stores are retail stores that sell a wide variety of inexpensive household goods at reduced prices. The stores are strategically located for your convenience. Their selling point is you can be in and out in the time it takes to find a parking spot at a superstore. Today the stores are thriving, opening hundreds of new stores every year.

The concept of dollar stores had its roots in the five-and-dime stores of the fifties, or dime stores as we called them. My parents liked to shop the dime stores in Cambridge. If my brothers and I behaved, we received a treat at Kresge's lunch counter – a dish of mashed potatoes with gravy.

I remember three dime stores in Cambridge – Kresge's, J.J. Newberry's, and F.W. Woolworth. I'm sure there were more, but the closest thing to a dime store in our area, other than the dollar stores, was a Ben Franklin store in Carrollton, Ohio.

Opioid Crisis: Is today's opioid crisis new, or has it existed for centuries? If we research history, we find many of our ancestors used opioids until they became illegal. Morphine was a drug given to wounded Civil War soldiers to ease their suffering. So many soldiers became addicted that it was called "The Army Disease." What was once, will be again.

Abuse of Power: The recent explosion of sexual harassment charges against people in high positions has swept the nation from Hollywood to Washington D.C. People being abused by people in power is not new. Take a minute to research the lives of some of our founding fathers. What you find will shock you. The abuse of power isn't new, just different people involved. So, the next time you see or hear of something new, stop and check it out. It may not be new at all.

Back in 1902...

| George Linn, of Columbus, is visiting his sister, Mrs. Hattie Smith. | Mrs. Walter Kennedy is on the sick list. |
| Mrs. Ella Wyrick was visiting relatives in Cambridge last Friday. | T. A. Johnston sold a bunch of fat sheep to William Thomas last week. |

One-sentence newsfeeds once went into the newspaper instead of onto Twitter. If you visited a relative, that was newsworthy. If you caught a bad cold, that was, too. Bought a new wagon? Sold some nice fat sheep? Put it in the paper. Enquiring minds wanted to know!

The Place to Be

BY BETSY TAYLOR

A bookworm's paradise.

Scientists tell us that memories are most strongly evoked by the sense of smell. For me, that's true of the aroma that greets readers when they enter a library. I think it's the scent of aged paper and the combination of odors embedded in old fabric book covers that seep into the air over time.

When I was seven years old and lived three blocks from the Guernsey County District Public Library, I marched in all by myself and got my first library card. A child could do that then. It's not so easy now and that's prudent. The "library lady" instructed me to print my name on the top line and my address on the next line of a white index card. She stepped to an old manual typewriter, struck a few keys, and handed me one of the best gifts ever. We had just begun studying cursive in second grade and my "legal" signature on the card couldn't have held up to scrutiny. But, there it was, on a small blue cardstock paper that I guarded with my life.

A children's room off to the left of the main desk boasted palatial ceilings and more books than I could count. I was euphoric! But the best thing was that I could borrow five books for **twenty-eight** days. On top of all that, the loan was FREE!

It hadn't always been that way. In 1898, when Mrs. J.D. Taylor started the library, lifetime memberships were sold for $25.00 each. Nonmembers paid a two-cents per day charge to use the library. The money went to buy books and rent a room on Wheeling Avenue donated by her husband, the Honorable J.D. Taylor. In 1901, the daily charge was dropped so that everyone could enjoy the library.

Most people in Cambridge are aware that ours is a Carnegie library. Andrew Carnegie provided funds for its construction. The City of Cambridge provided land, books, and the promise to set aside money for operating expenses. The current building opened in 1901 and, to my delight, looks almost the same today.

Over time, our library evolved. It became a school district library in 1923, opened a branch in Byesville in 1936, became a county district library in 1948, and built the Crossroads Branch Library in 2006. In 1958, the first ever bookmobile was purchased with federal funds and it was ours!

Library evolution hasn't only been about bigger, better, newer buildings, and books. It has also been about public services. Remember microfiche film rolls? What a space saver! Most of us don't remember a library without audiovisual services. Today the computer stations are always crowded. How about a dedicated section that caters to genealogic research? Book club and elementary reading sponsorship is an educational and social boon to our community.

Our library is a welcoming environment in which to hold fun events, meetings, and informational sessions. If you haven't taken advantage of all that waits inside, you're really missing out.

The seven-year-old me could never have imagined how much I would enjoy and depend on our library system throughout my childhood and into adulthood. Not once have I ever let my precious library card lapse.

Although I don't remember her name, I recall her curly cinnamon-colored hair and thick glasses. She was the library lady who ushered me into the place to be and I say, "Thank you."

An Old Map's Story...

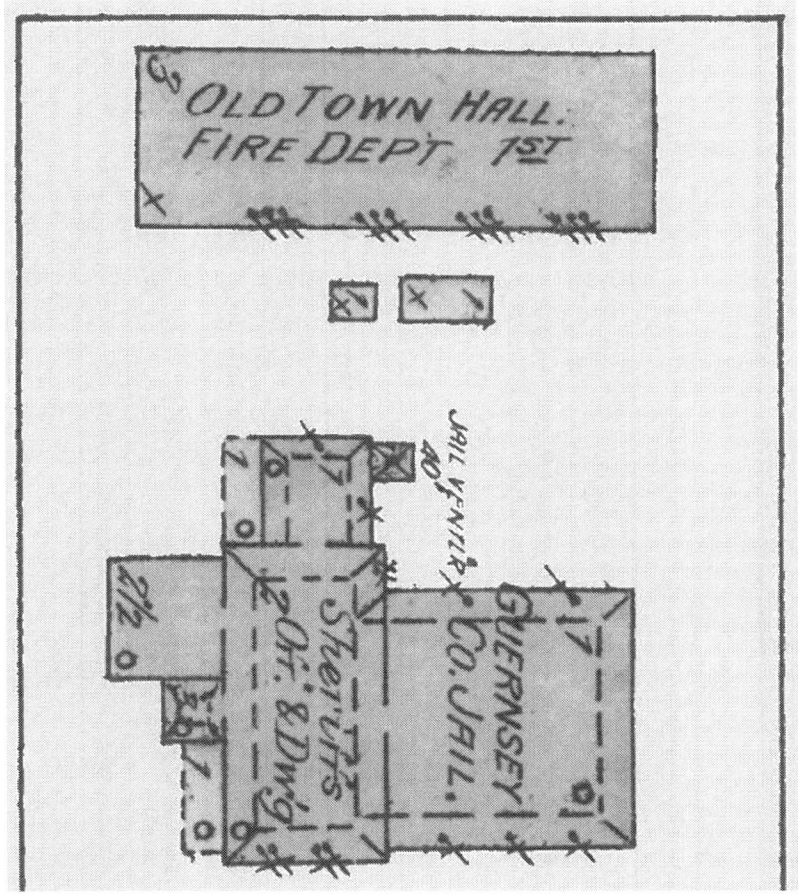

Before the Guernsey County Library was built in 1903, its site on Steubenville Avenue had once been occupied by the three-story Cambridge "Old Town Hall." An 1886 map shows the county jail and sheriff's office behind the hall, where today there is only a parking lot.

What Happened to "Bill"?

BY BOB LEY

It's about your moniker, namely.

Sometimes the "old-fashioned" names are comforting to hear in this time of turmoil. Those names most often carried a nickname tied to them. Somehow, it seemed easier to relate to a Bill, Tom, or Fred. They seemed to be one of us.

Check out the 'New Babies' edition of the paper around January of each year, and notice how few traditional names you see. Sports fans will attest to the plethora of "original" names of today. Discounting religious names, *Mohammed*, for example, and national names, like the runner, *Usain* Bolt, we still notice a long list of unusual first names. I am sure the athletes' parents couldn't care less about what anyone thinks of the names, which is their right.

Disapproval is not my intention. I certainly would not want *Vadal, NaVorro, Denico,* or *Carderelle* (all Raiders) to be upset with me. The names make me wonder why *Alshon's* or *Mychal's* (the Eagles) parents would choose to name their offspring something the child would need to spell and explain hundreds of times in a lifetime.

Cedi, London, and *LeBron* (all Cavs) are more names new to me, as are *Jabari* and *Kyrie* of the Celtics. Don't you wonder what their nicknames would be?

Is the time spent spelling

it out or pronouncing it worth the individualism? It reminds me of the television commercial:

Lady behind the counter asks the man, "Are you really Christopher Paul Bacon?"

"Yes, ma'am," he says.

"So you're *Crispy Bacon!*"

There are many more intriguing first names. And contrary to the tone of this, they are not exclusive to present day. In 1806, Cambridge's Founders Cemetery was platted by one *Zaccheus* Beatty, a name that even then probably was not common!

It's at least as different as *Yonder* of the Cleveland Indians or *Tyrann*, an Arizona Cardinal. Next time you watch a televised sport, look at the various player's names. You'll find it fascinating.

Me? Give me a "Bill" any day!

A Mysterious Name...

FRANCIS DONSONCHET
FRENCH SOLDIER
SERVED IN
NAPOLEON BONAPARTE'S
ARMY

There are at least three different spellings in historical records for the name of one of Napoleon's soldiers buried in Founders' Cemetery: Donsonchet, Donsouchet, and Dousouchet. None of these names is known elsewhere. He was likely a "Dusonchet" instead.

My Own Little Miracle

BY JUDY SIMCOX

In Providence we trust.

Some scales fell from my eyes that Sunday. Let me tell you. I do believe in miracles. I was making a batch of Christmas cookies on a Saturday afternoon, washing up the mixing bowl, when I noticed my wedding ring was missing. I had lost some weight in the summer and fall, and with the dry air of winter affecting my hands, my ring had slipped off. It had happened before, but the ring always made a "clinking" sound, so I would stop to look for it.

I looked in the dishwater, and down the disposal with an LED light. The disposal was out of order, so no danger of grinding. I even pinched and poked through the lump of dough I had chilling in the fridge. I was upset, but I am not generally given to hysteria. My husband's ring had fallen off due to the same two factors, and I had been able to find it. I could find mine.

I looked in jeans pockets and jacket pockets, and down in the pertinent finger of my glove. I looked around the car, the seat and the door pocket, where I had been tucking little gift purchases as I acquired them. I also looked in the cushions of the couch. There was only one more place I wanted to look, but I would have to wait for morning. I spent the night thinking I could find my grandmother's gold band, which I had stored in a box somewhere, and have it sized up, if it came to that.

I went to Sunday school the next morning, but found I was so agitated, I skipped church and went to K-Mart. I had been there the day before, and while putting a sack in the back seat, noticed a bag of stale bread I'd had in the car for a while, intending to toss to the ducks at the city pond. The feisty sparrows who lurk around the K-Mart parking lot had been exploring for crumbs, so I threw some bread to them. Soon that startling flock of gulls that swoop from the waters by the railroad tracks showed up, and chased off the smaller birds. I decided to scatter the rest of the bread on the grassy edge next to the pavement, for come-who-will. I sat in the car and cast handfuls of bread onto the grass until it was gone, and I drove home.

A little snow had fallen in the night, but I thought such a light dusting might highlight an artificial shape, like my ring. I parked the car next to the gravelly edge, and began to walk back and forth over the grass. I thought that by tossing the bread, my ring could have flown ten feet. I was about to give up when, looking at my feet in the gravel, there it was . . . just inches away. It was indeed highlighted by the snow.

I picked up the ring, still not sure it was mine. Like someone else might have lost a gold band there. Then everything got lighter, like the sun had come out of the clouds, which it hadn't. I had left church by the back door to cover this last searching possibility, but I felt the only place to go at that moment was back to church, and the only One to tell was the Lord. I was standing at the back of the church taking off my coat when I saw the microphone was being passed around for testimonies, so I testified – a first for me. I was, and I am, very happy and blessed.

RDW

Way Back in 1930...

EVER READY CAB
15 Cents

Service and Comfort
SPECIAL TRIPS
Hour Work

OPPOSITE BUS TERMINAL
PHONE 2429

Durable Dentistry. Moderate Prices. Warranted Work.

The Easy Way

DR. PURDUM
831 Wheeling Ave.

FIREPLACE
INN and TEA ROOM
TWO MILES WEST OF CAMBRIDGE
Ohio U. S. Route 40
Phone R 44Y4

Mr. and Mrs. Lyman M. Shafer

ATKINS--The Jeweler
Authorized Distributor

Bluebird Registered
DIAMOND RINGS
AND
GRUEN WATCHES

OPPOSITE COURT HOUSE

Ads in a 1930 Colonial Theater program promoted 15-cent cab rides, dentures, a cozy place to eat, and the Atkins jewelry store for rings.

Photo courtesy of the Guernsey County History Museum.

Church at Seneca Lake

BY BOB LEY

Mass en masse.

Sunday Mass was always a part of my life, and having children made it even more important to me. My wife and I made every effort to get there as a family.

We had an old cabin at Seneca Lake and it was our summertime headquarters. Boating was our family summer pastime. It was something each of us could participate in as a family, regardless of age. During our first years at the lake, Lore City was the closest church for us to go to Mass.

With the opening of the church on State Route 313, the trip to church was more convenient. The church's interior boasted a beautiful beamed ceiling. The really nice thing was that on Sundays, when it was practical, Mass was held outside on the lawn behind the church. It was all so casual, even the kids looked forward to going. Occasionally a group of motorcyclists would ride by, drowning out the priest for a minute, but for the most part, having Mass outdoors seemed like getting to know nature better.

We would gather in loose groups in the yard afterward, introducing ourselves to visitors from all over. It was incredible how many states were represented on any given Sunday.

I am not sure why the church was later closed. Perhaps attendance was considered insufficient to sustain it. Maybe finding a priest who would be available was the problem. Perhaps funding for the short season and paying for the building also played a role.

Eventually the building was sold. A family made it into their home and it looks very nice from the outside. I have never seen the inside since its conversion, but I can imagine how beautiful it must be with those grand beams holding up the ceiling for an open floor plan.

My family and I are sure many others enjoyed attending church there.

Trial by Fire...

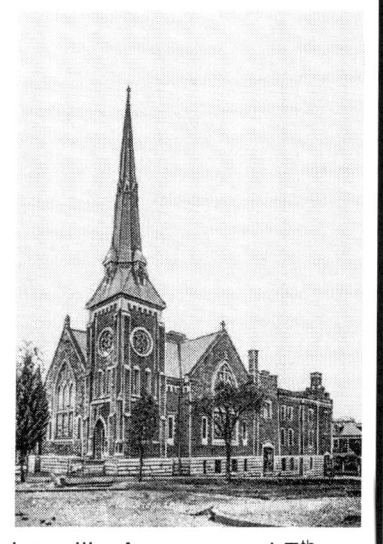

The Methodist Church at the corner of Steubenville Avenue and 7th Street has an unusual cornerstone. It says "Erected 1885. Rebuilt 1898." A fire on November 27th, 1897, destroyed much of the then 12-year-old church, but left its walls standing. On the second anniversary of the fire, it reopened. The picture at left shows the fire's damage; at right is the church's appearance on a 1909 postcard. In 2012, rare hundred-mile-per-hour straight line winds caused extensive, expensive damage to the structure, yet still it survives.

Photos courtesy of the Guernsey County History Museum.

I'm from Buffalo

BY SAMUEL D. BESKET

Thumbing my way across the USA.

Hitchhiking, also known as riding your thumb or simply thumbing, is a means of transportation that has existed for decades. It means asking strangers for a ride in their vehicle, and it was used by everyone, young and old alike. Not everyone had an automobile, or could afford one.

Hitchhiking peaked in the '70s, then declined due to the low cost of travel and more access to automobiles. The building of the interstate highway system dealt the final blow. With limited access and questionable individuals traveling the roads, people were reluctant to accept or give a ride to a stranger.

If you lived in Guernsey County in the '50s, seeing hitchhikers standing along the road was a common sight. Getting a ride was easy. The people who picked you up usually knew you, and you knew them. A popular hitchhiking spot in Cambridge was located on East Wheeling Avenue by the Ford Garage.

My first experience with hitchhiking occurred when several of us boys decided to hitch a ride to the beach at Seneca Lake. That was the beginning of years of thumbing that covered several states.

It served me well while I was in the Air Force. Getting a ride was easy in 1963, because people were willing to give a young man in uniform a lift. My rides were with young college girls, a grandmother who had two grandsons serving in the

Army, and a salesman who let me drive his new Thunderbird.

By far the best rides were with truck drivers. They were driving long distances anyway, and could connect you with other truck drivers going the same direction. On one occasion, my ride took me to a truck stop in Dayton. The truck driver bought me an early breakfast, then stood on a chair and announced, "Anyone going east on Route 40? This young trooper needs a ride." Immediately, a man shouted he was going to Uniontown, Pennsylvania. Fifteen hours after leaving my base, I was home.

My most unusual ride happened when a truck driver picked me up in Toledo.

"Where you going?" he asked.

"About 90 miles east of Columbus."

"What's the town?"

"Cambridge."

"You live in Cambridge?"

"No, I live in a little town called Lore City. Not many people have heard of it."

He chuckled, stuck out his hand, and said, "I'm from Buffalo."

The last time I was involved in hitchhiking was to help a homesick soldier return to his base. In order to tell this story, we must fast forward twenty years to the eighties.

Bob, the shift superintendent, and I were working third shift at our factory when we saw a stranger standing by the entrance door. As we approached him, I asked, "Can we help you?"

"Just getting warm," he replied.

"Are you traveling?" Bob chimed in.

"Trying to get to Queens, New York, for Thanksgiving," he added. After we exchanged puzzled looks, Bob asked, "Are you military?"

The young man just stared at the floor for a few minutes, then looked up, "I was, but I quit."

"You don't just quit," Bob interjected. "Did you walk away from your post?"

After a few agonizing seconds, the young man nodded his head yes.

"Where is your post?"

"Fort Sill, Oklahoma. It sure is different from Queens."

"Why don't we have a cup of coffee and talk about this?" Bob said.

After several cups of coffee, Bob was able to convince the young man it was in his best interest to return to his post. We arranged a ride for him to Iowa in one of our company trucks. Gary, the driver, said he would get him a ride south once they got there. True to his word, Gary told us later he hooked him up with a driver going to Missouri.

Seeing how Bob handled this delicate situation greatly increased my respect for him. He could have called the police and been done with it. Instead, he chose to bend a few rules to help a homesick soldier find his way.

This photograph shows Valley Regional High School, also known as Buffalo High School, as pictured in the school's 1948 yearbook. There were 18 freshmen, 14 sophomores, 19 juniors, and 16 graduating seniors that year.

A SPECIAL NOTE OF THANKS

The Guernsey County History Museum, 218 N. 8th St., Cambridge

Guernsey County is rich in history, reaching back more than two centuries. The Guernsey County Historical Society has accordingly been collecting and displaying mementos of that history at their museum on North Eighth Street in Cambridge since the 1960s. It has also recently begun digitizing historical photos and documents for display online, primarily in their Flickr photo collection, accessible at www.guernseycountyhistory.com, the Museum's website. Many of the filler photos between articles in this book come from that repository. The Museum invites the public to learn more about Guernsey County's history by visiting them either on site or online.

The Rainy Day Writers give special thanks to the Guernsey County History Museum for their photo gems lent to this book.

Made in the USA
Columbia, SC
14 October 2018